the
Chinese
Classroom

book 2

first steps in reading and writing

蔡华
Hua Cai

LEXUS

Published 2008 by Lexus Ltd
60 Brook Street, Glasgow G40 2AB
www.lexusforlanguages.co.uk

Editors:
李钊 Li Zhao
Tom Mitford

Design and typesetting: Elfreda Crehan
Artwork: Elfreda Crehan and Sharon Scotland
Photographs: 朱卫静 Weijing Zhu
General editor: Peter Terrell

The voices on the website download are:
尹英旭 Yingxu Yin
Peter Terrell
Jeremy Butterfield

British Library Cataloguing in Publication Data
A catalogue record for this book is available from the British Library.

ISBN 978-1-904737-148

Printed and bound in Malta by the Gutenberg Press

Contents

Introduction

Chinese script has a widespread reputation for being fiendishly complex. A fresh new English student of Chinese, about to start his studies, was once told: *so you want to learn Chinese, well the script is difficult — and it gets harder.*

Well now, step into the Chinese Classroom, Book 2 and enjoy a gentle yet thorough introduction to this amazing and totally different form of written communication.

How to use this book

This introduction to Chinese and Chinese script (in what is known as the simplified version) is made up of 63 lessons spread over 4 blocks. The lessons are short and consist, in the main, of

- ✓ a vocabulary list with characters
- ✓ (in Blocks 1 and 2) guidelines on how to write these characters
- ✓ exercises to develop familiarity
- ✓ cartoons, puzzles and quizzes

Sometimes the Chinese characters are accompanied by both English translations and pinyin (the way of writing Chinese using the roman alphabet). And sometimes, for example where the characters are given as captions to pictures, the English is left out, since the meaning will be clear enough just by looking at the pictures.

As you work through this book, you'll be encouraged to write the characters down and also to say the Chinese out loud. This all goes to reinforce the memorizing process.

Use the Answers section to see how you're doing with the exercises. But if you're not sure of an answer to a question, try not to dive straight into the Answers section. Search back in the book or get used to working with the three glossaries at the end of the book.

The general rules of stroke order

Here are some general guidelines about writing Chinese.

A horizontal line is drawn before a vertical line.

A left-falling stroke goes before a right-falling stroke.

Start at the top and work down to the bottom.

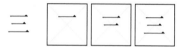

Go from left to right.

Go from outside to inside.

Inside strokes precede the closing stroke.

The middle stroke comes before the two sides.

How to pronounce the Chinese in this book

Log on to www.lexusforlanguages.co.uk and you will be able to listen to a Chinese voice reading all the vocabulary in this book. You can download this in mp3 format.

Here are the main points to remember about pinyin.

a	as in f*a*ther
ai	as in Th*ai*land
ao	like ow in c*ow*
c	ts
chi	chur
ci	tsur
e	as in h*e*r
ei	as in *ei*ght
en	as in op*en*
eng	like *en* in op*en* plus g
i	as in maga*zi*ne (except after c, ch, r, s, sh, z & zh)
ian	similar to *yen*
ie	like ye in *ye*s
iu	like yo in *yo*ga
ju	the u is like a French u
o	as in m*o*re
ong	oong with oo as in s*oo*n
ou	as in d*ou*gh
q	like ch in *ch*eap
qu	the u is like a French u
ri	rur
shi	shur
si	sur
u	as in r*u*le (except after j, q and x)
ua	w followed by *a* (above)
uai	similar to *why*
ue	ü (below) followed by e as in l*e*t
ui	similar to *way*

un	like uan in tr*uan*t
uo	similar to *war*
ü	as in French t*u* or German *ü*ber
x	like sh in *sh*eep, with the lips spread as in a smile
xu	the u is like a French u
z	like ds in bi*ds*
zh	like j in *j*udo
zhi	jur
zi	dzur

Tones

Chinese has four tones, as well as what is known as a 'light tone' or 'neutral tone' - which is when no tone mark is given. The four tones are:

A change in tone brings a change in meaning. For example:

jī	*first tone*	chicken		jǐ	*third tone*	how many
jí	*second tone*	extremely		jì	*fourth tone*	to send

Tones in English?

In a sense, you can think of spoken English as having tones as well. Only in English these tones will express an attitude on the part of the speaker and don't have an impact on the actual meaning of a word. They will indicate, for instance, whether the speaker is expressing doubt or making a definite assertion or showing surprise. Here are some examples of tone-like occurrences in English.

Everybody smile please, say **CHEESE**	*cheese is first tone*
You did **WHAT?**	*what is second tone*
Let me think, *umm...*	*umm is third tone*
I said **NO!**	*no is fourth tone*

Block 1

Lesson 1 ~ *Numbers*

*T*his book is all about reading and writing, so why don't we start off with some arithmetic. In this first lesson we're going to learn a group of simple hanzi (Chinese characters): the numbers from one to ten.

一	yī	one
二	èr	two
三	sān	three
四	sì	four
五	wǔ	five
六	liù	six
七	qī	seven
八	bā	eight
九	jiǔ	nine
十	shí	ten

character building

Each of these characters (apart from the first) is made up of several strokes written in a set sequence, normally going from top to bottom and left to right. Copy these strokes in the empty boxes beneath each line so as to make up these characters for yourself. Say the Chinese out loud as you do this.

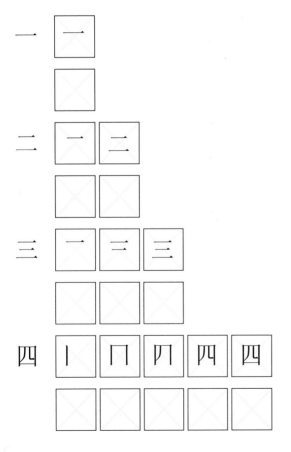

五　一　丁　五　五

六　丶　亠　亠　六

七　乚　七

八　丿　八

九　乁　九

十　一　十

Exercise 1

Which character in each of these groups is not a number?

1) 五 七 八 大 ....

2) 九 八 人 一 ....

3) 二 四 回 六 ....

4) 三 丰 七 八 ....

5) 力 九 十 七 ....

Exercise 2

Write out these characters so as to go from the lowest number to the highest. Say the words out loud when you do this.

1) 三 一 四 二 ....

2) 五 九 三 七 ....

3) 二 七 五 十 ....

4) 八 三 六 九 ....

5) 四 十 九 一 ....

Exercise 3

Rearrange these characters so as to go from the highest number to the lowest. Say the words out loud when you do this.

1) 八 一 十 二 ....
2) 三 九 一 四 ....
3) 六 十 五 七 ....
4) 二 八 七 三 ....
5) 一 九 六 五 ....

Exercise 4

Write the Chinese character in the empty box.

1) sì (4)

2) wǔ (5)

3) qī (7)

4) bā (8)

5) jiǔ (9)

Exercise 5

Write the Chinese character which comes immediately after each of the following. Say the word out loud.

1) 五

2) 八

3) 二

4) 三

5) 九

Exercise 6

Write the Chinese character which comes immediately before each of the following. Say the word out loud.

1) ☐ 三

2) ☐ 十

3) ☐ 五

4) ☐ 二

5) ☐ 七

Lesson 2 ~ *Simple arithmetic*

In this lesson we are going to do some more exercises to get familiar with the ten numbers that you have now learned.

You'll need to know these additional characters:

加	jiā	plus
减	jiǎn	minus
等 于	děng yú	equals

Exercise 1

Choose the correct answer from the three options given in brackets. Write your answer in the empty box. And say the sums out loud.

1) 二 加 五 等于 ☐ （ 六， 七， 八 ）

2) 七 加 一 等于 ☐ （ 六， 七， 八 ）

3) 三 加 四 等于 ☐ （ 十， 六， 七 ）

4) 十 减 六 等于 ☐ （ 四， 五， 三 ）

5) 八 减 二 等于 ☐ （ 四， 五， 六 ）

Exercise 2

Circle the odd man out in each group of characters.

1) 一 六 十 太

2) 三 十 丰 四

3) 九 为 七 八

4) 木 十 五 六

5) 七 五 丸 六

Lesson 2

Exercise 3

Addition. Do these simple sums, saying the Chinese out loud.

1) 四 加 三 等于 ☐

2) 六 加 二 等于 ☐

3) 一 加 九 等于 ☐

4) 二 加 三 等于 ☐

5) 四 加 五 等于 ☐

Exercise 4

Subtraction. Do these sums, saying the Chinese out loud.

1) 十 减 一 等于 ☐

2) 七 减 三 等于 ☐

3) 六 减 三 等于 ☐

4) 十 减 八 等于 ☐

5) 八 减 三 等于 ☐

Exercise 5

Write the answers to these sums in the empty boxes.
Remember to say the Chinese out loud.

1) 二 加 六 减 一 等于 ☐

2) 七 加 二 减 四 等于 ☐

3) 四 加 五 减 七 等于 ☐

4) 三 加 六 减 一 等于 ☐

5) 六 加 四 减 一 等于 ☐

Well done.
You're now getting used to reading and working with some Chinese characters.

Lesson 3 ~ *More numbers*

In this lesson we are going to learn how to work with some more numbers. Look at the following examples and see if you can identify the regular rule to form numbers from 11 to 99.

十	shí	10	二十一	èr shí yī	21
十一	shí yī	11	二十二	èr shí èr	22
十二	shí èr	12	三十	sān shí	30
十三	shí sān	13	三十一	sān shí yī	31
二十	èr shí	20	三十二	sān shí èr	32

Exercise 1

Now you write the Chinese characters and the pinyin (or Chinese written in the roman alphabet) for the following numbers.

1) 40 ....

2) 50 ....

3) 60 ....

4) 70 ....

5) 80 ....

6) 85 ....

7) 90 ....

Now let's do some more exercises to get familiar with these characters. You'll need to know these additional characters:

乘以 chéng yǐ   multiplied by

除以 chú yǐ   divided by

and remember

等于 děng yú   equals

Exercise 2

Choose the correct answer from the three options given in brackets. And say the sums out loud.

1) 三 乘以 五 等于 . . . .
（ 十六, 十五, 十四 ）

2) 二 乘以 九 等于 . . . .
（ 十八, 十九, 二十 ）

3) 四 乘以 十 等于 . . . .
（ 三十, 十四, 四十 ）

4) 八 乘以 九 等于 . . . .
（ 二十七, 七十三, 七十二 ）

5) 六 除以 二 等于 . . . .
（ 二, 三, 四 ）

6) 十二 除以 三 等于 . . . .
（ 六, 五, 四 ）

7) 二十二 除以 二 等于 . . . .
（ 十, 十一, 十二 ）

8) 五十六 除以 八 等于 . . . .
（ 六, 七, 八 ）

Exercise 3

Can you do these multiplication sums?

1) 四 乘以 三 等于 . . . .

2) 五 乘以 六 等于 . . . .

3) 九 乘以 五 等于 . . . .

4) 十一 乘以 六 等于 . . . .

5) 二十 乘以 四 等于 . . . .

6) 十五 乘以 五 等于 . . . .

7) 二十四 乘以 三 等于 . . . .

8) 四十三 乘以 二 等于 . . . .

Exercise 4

Can you do these division sums?

1) 九 除以 三 等于 . . . .

2) 十 除以 二 等于 . . . .

3) 十六 除以 八 等于 . . . .

4) 二十七 除以 三 等于 . . . .

5) 三十 除以 二 等于 . . . .

6) 四十二 除以 七 等于 . . . .

7) 五十 除以 二 等于 . . . .

8) 八十 除以 十 等于 . . . .

Fill in the empty squares to make the numbers add up to the same total in each direction. You should not use the same number more than once.

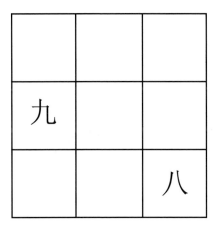

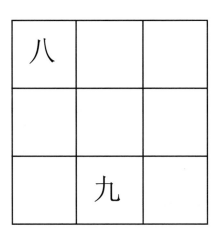

Lesson 4 ~ *Bigger numbers*

*I*n this lesson we are going to learn how to deal with some bigger numbers.

百	bǎi	hundred
千	qiān	thousand
万	wàn	ten thousand
亿	yì	hundred million

character building

百	一	一	丆	百	百	百

千	一	二	千

万	一	丆	万

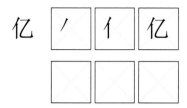

You'll see that Chinese doesn't have a unit corresponding to a million. Instead Chinese says 百万 (which means literally: a hundred ten thousands).

Neither does Chinese have a unit corresponding to a billion. Chinese says 十亿 (which means literally: ten hundred millions).

The pinyin words for 'one' and 'hundred million' are very similar: **yī** and **yì**. But the characters are VERY different.

Now, study the following examples and say them out loud. Notice that Chinese doesn't use a word for 'and'. But there are differences in the way numbers are written and said. These have been highlighted for you.

You will also need to know this character:

零 líng zero

一百	yì bǎi	100
一百零一	yì bǎi líng yī	101
一百一十	yì bǎi yī shí	110
一百一十一	yì bǎi yī shí yī	111
一百二十	yì bǎi èr shí	120
一百二十一	yì bǎi èr shí yī	121
二百	èr bǎi	200
二百零一	èr bǎi líng yī	201
二百一十	èr bǎi yī shí	210
二百一十一	èr bǎi yī shí yī	211
二百二十	èr bǎi èr shí	220
二百二十一	èr bǎi èr shí yī	221
一千	yì qiān	1000
一千零一	yì qiān líng yī	1001
一千一百	yì qiān yì bǎi	1100
一千一百一十	yì qiān yì bǎi yī shí	1110
一千一百一十一	yì qiān yì bǎi yī shí yī	1111

In normal speech **yī** changes to **yì** in combinations like these.

Exercise 1

Underline the correct answer by choosing from the three possibilities for each question.

1) 二百三十 加 五 等于

（ 二百三十六， 二百三十七， 二百三十五 ）

2) 一百六十二 加 三十四 等于

（ 一百九十六， 一百九十七， 一百九十八 ）

3) 四百五十七 加 三 等于

（ 四百一十六， 四百六十， 四百六十八 ）

4) 二百零五 减 五 等于

（ 二百， 二百零二， 二百零一 ）

5) 五百二十三 减 二十 等于

（ 五百， 五百零二， 五百零三 ）

6) 二百一十九 减 十六 等于

（ 二百一十， 二百一十二， 二百零三 ）

Exercise 2

Circle the odd man out.

1) 百 白 千 万
2) 千 万 方 亿
3) 百 干 万 亿
4) 千 万 乙 百
5) 百 于 十 千
6) 亿 万 力 百

Exercise 3

Write the Chinese characters for the pinyin.

1) èr bǎi yì shí sì . . . .

2) yì qiān jiǔ bǎi wǔ shí liù . . . .

3) qī wàn bā qiān yì bǎi liù shí sān . . . .

4) èr bǎi qī shí bā wàn sì qiān wǔ bǎi

. . . .

5) jiǔ qiān sān bǎi èr shí sì . . . .

6) shí wàn bā qiān . . . .

Lesson 5 ~ *Directions*

In this lesson we are going to look at some basic direction words.

东	dōng	east
西	xī	west
南	nán	south
北	běi	north

Character building

东	一	𠂉	车	东	东	
西	一	丆	冂	丙	襾	西

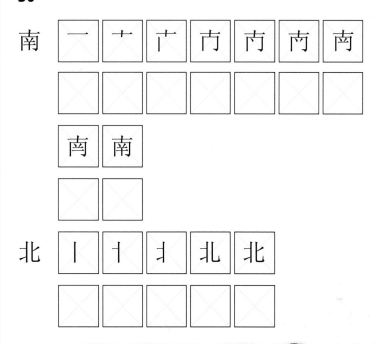

Use 东北 or 西南 rather than 北东 or 南西 to express 'northeast' and 'southwest'.

Normally we need to combine the direction words with 在 **zài** and 边 **biān** to describe the specific direction. For example, 在北边 means 'in the north'.

New hanzi

在	zài	at, in, on; with sense of be (be at, be in, be on)
边	biān	side

 *character building*

在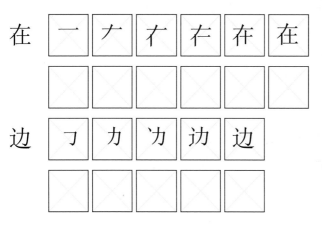

边

Exercise 1

Study the following map and choose the correct answer from the four possibilities for each question. Say each answer out loud and write the characters in the space provided.

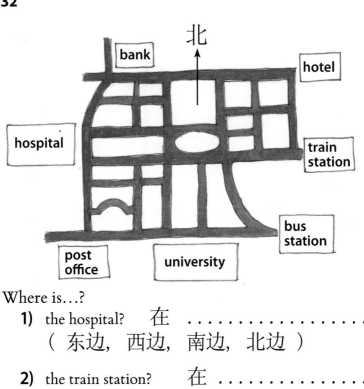

Where is…?

1) the hospital? 在 ....
（ 东边， 西边， 南边， 北边 ）

2) the train station? 在 ....
（ 东边， 西边， 南边， 北边 ）

3) the university? 在 ....
（ 东边， 西边， 南边， 北边 ）

4) the hotel? 在 ....
（ 东南， 北东， 东北， 西北 ）

5) the bank? 在 ....
（ 东南， 西南， 北西， 西北 ）

6) the bus station? 在 ....
（ 西南， 东南， 北西， 西北 ）

7) the post office? 在 . . . .

（ 南西， 西南， 北西， 西北 ）

Exercise 2

Read the following sentences and fill in each numbered box with the English name for what is located there.

The supermarket 在 cinema 北边.

The park 在 cinema 南边.

The restaurant 在 cinema 东边.

The gym 在 cinema 西边.

The hotel 在 cinema 西北.

The airport 在 cinema 东南.

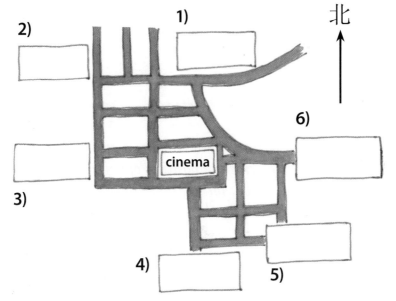

Exercise 3

Fill in the empty stroke sequence boxes to form a complete character.

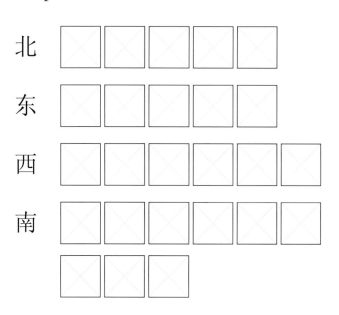

Lesson 6 ~ *Positions*

*I*n this lesson we are going to learn a group of characters to describe the position of things. We will learn words to describe, for example, whether something is on or under something else. Here is the new hanzi list.

上	shàng	on
下	xià	under
左	zuǒ	left
右	yòu	right

Character building

上 | 丨 | 卜 | 上 |

下 | 一 | 丁 | 下 |

左 | 一 | 一 | 一 | 左 | 左 |

右 | 一 | 一 | 才 | 右 | 右 |

As we have mentioned before, when speaking of positions or directions, we normally need to add the hanzi 在 and 边 to describe the position or direction. For example, 在…上 or 在…右边.

Exercise 1

Study the pictures below and write out the correct answers.

1) The pen 在 desk (上, 下, 左边, 右边)

....

2) The pen 在 cup (上, 下, 左边, 右边)

....

3) The book 在 floor (上, 下, 左边, 右边)

....

4) The book 在 desk （ 上，下， 左边， 右边 ）

· ·

5) The cup 在 desk （ 上，下， 左边， 右边 ）

· ·

6) The café 在 the theatre （ 左边， 右边 ）

· ·

7) The theatre 在 the café （ 左边， 右边 ）

· ·

Exercise 2

Circle the odd man out.

1) 上 右 卞

2) 左 右 土

3) 左 石 上

Exercise 3

Draw a line to connect each character with its correct pinyin form.

1) 左   biān

2) 上   zuǒ

3) 东   xī

4) 边   yòu

5) 在   shàng

6) 右   dōng

7) 西   zài

Lesson 7 ~ *More positions*

*W*e're now going to learn a few more of these position words.

里	lǐ	in
外	wài	outside
前	qián	front
后	hòu	back
在 … 前 边	zài … qián biān	in front of
在 … 后 边	zài … hòu biān	behind

Lesson 7

Character building

里 | 丨 | 冂 | 日 | 旦 | 甲 | 甲 | 里 |

外 | ノ | ク | 夕 | 列 | 外 |

前 | 丶 | 丷 | 丷 | 产 | 前 | 前 | 前 |
前 | 前 |

后 | 一 | 厂 | 厅 | 斤 | 后 | 后 |

Exercise 1

Study the following pictures and then write out the Chinese
characters which correctly complete each sentence.

1) The pen 在 drawer . . . .
（ 左边， 右边， 里边， 外边 ）

2) The book 在 desk . . . .
（ 上， 下， 里边， 外边 ）

3) The book 在 drawer . . . .
（ 左边， 右边， 里边， 外边 ）

4) The chair 在 desk . . . .
（ 前边， 后边， 里边， 外边 ）

5) The desk 在 chair . . . .
（ 前边， 后边， 里边， 外边 ）

6) The pond 在 the park . . . .

（ 左边， 右边， 里边， 外边 ）

7) The tree 在 the pond . . . .

（ 左边， 右边， 里边， 外边 ）

8) The flowers 在 the tree . . . .

（ 左边， 右边， 里边， 外边 ）

9) The cafe 在 the pond . . . .

（ 前边， 后边， 里边， 外边 ）

10) The dog 在 the cafe . . . .

（ 左边， 右边， 里边， 外边 ）

11) The duck 在 the pond . . . .

（ 左边， 右边， 里边， 外边 ）

Lesson 7

Exercise 2

Draw a line to connect each pinyin word with its character.

1) nán   里

2) běi   边

3) zài   后

4) biān   南

5) wài   北

6) qián   在

7) lǐ   外

8) hòu   前

Exercise 3

Choose the character with the most strokes in each group. Write it down and say it out loud.

1) 东 西 右 北
2) 百 前 上 下
3) 后 里 外 左
4) 千 万 右 十
5) 南 里 西 亿

Lesson 8 ~ *Parts of the body*

*I*n this lesson we are going to learn some simple characters for parts of the body.

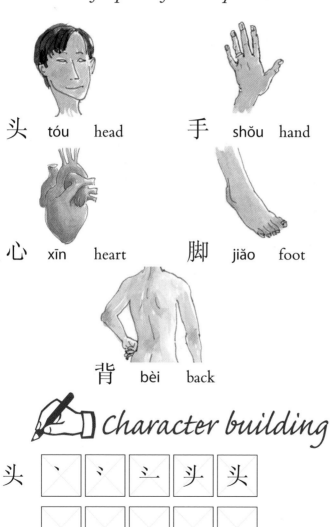

头 tóu head   手 shǒu hand

心 xīn heart   脚 jiǎo foot

背 bèi back

character building

头 | 丶 | 丷 | 头 | 头 | 头

手 | 一 | 二 | 三 | 手

心 | 丶 | 心 | 心 | 心

脚 | 丿 | 刀 | 月 | 月 | 尸 | 尸 | 尸 | 尸

胩 | 脚 | 脚

背 | 丨 | 丬 | 긔 | 北 | 北 | 背 | 背

背 | 背

Now let's do some exercises.

Exercise 1

Circle the odd man out in each group.

1) 头　买　脚
2) 手　于　头
3) 心　必　脚
4) 背　北　头
5) 是　脚　手

Exercise 2

Write the appropriate Chinese character in each numbered box.

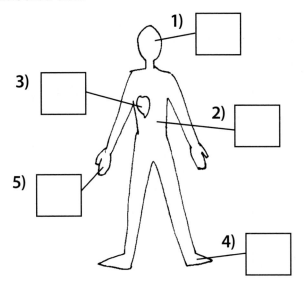

Lesson 9 ~ *Faces*

*I*n this lesson we're going to learn some basic
characters for describing a person's face.

脸 liǎn face   舌 shé tongue   耳 ěr ears

牙 yá teeth   下巴 xià ba chin   头发 tóu fà hair

 character building

脸 | 丿 | 刀 | 月 | 月 | 月 | 肜 | 胪 | 脸

脸 | 脸 | 脸

舌　| 一 | 二 | 千 | 千 | 舌 | 舌 |

耳　| 一 | 丆 | 丌 | 丏 | 耳 | 耳 |

牙　| 一 | 二 | 牙 | 牙 |

巴　| 𠃌 | 𠃍 | 𠃑 | 巴 |

发　| 乀 | 𠂇 | 龙 | 发 | 发 |

ěr can mean 'ear' or 'ears'; yá can mean 'teeth' or 'tooth'

Lesson 9

Now let's do some exercises.

Exercise 1

Circle the odd man out in each group.

1) 右 脚 舌 头   4) 月 牙 耳 舌

2) 耳 聂 手 心   5) 古 舌 发 牙

3) 牙 芽 心 舌

Exercise 2

Write the appropriate Chinese character in each numbered box.

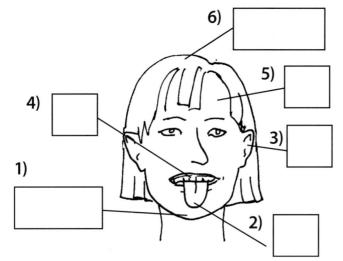

Exercise 3

The labelling for this body has gone all wrong. The
hanzi are in the right place. But the pronunciations in
pinyin are all jumbled up. Can you write the correct
pinyin for each part of the body?

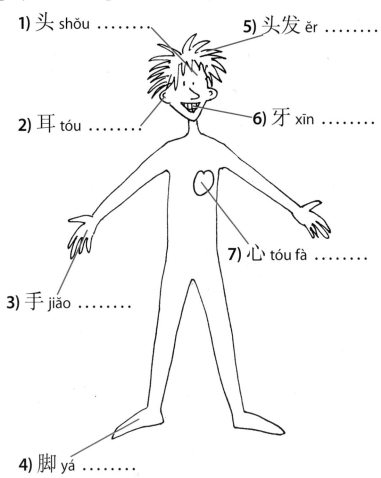

1) 头 shǒu ....

5) 头发 ěr ....

2) 耳 tóu ....

6) 牙 xīn ....

7) 心 tóu fà ....

3) 手 jiǎo ....

4) 脚 yá ....

Lesson 10 ~ *Telling the time*

In this lesson we are going to learn some characters for telling the time.

点	diǎn	o'clock
分	fēn	minute
小 时	xiǎo shí	hour
半	bàn	half past; half
几 点 了 ?	jǐ diǎn le?	what's the time?

小 is the Chinese for 'little'

Character building

点

丶	𠂆	广	占	占	卢	点

点	点

分

丿	八	分	分

小

时

半

几

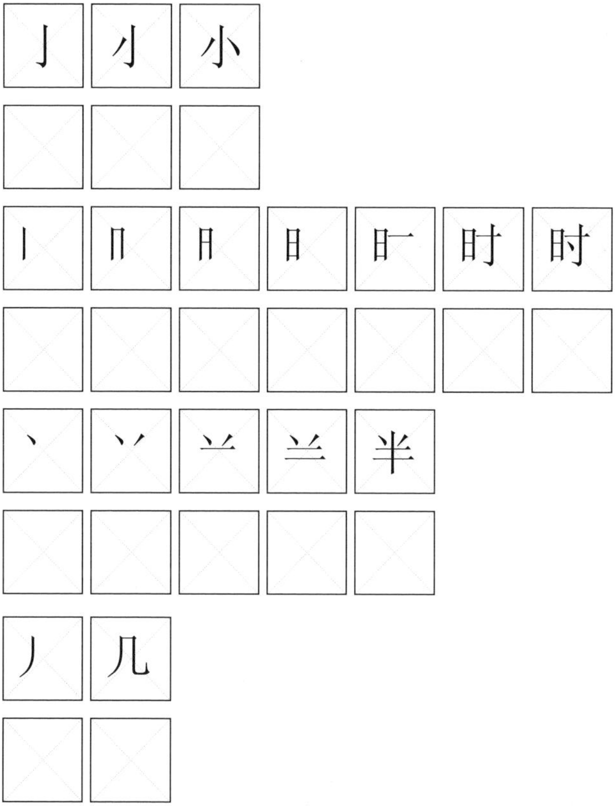

There are two ways of saying ‘half past …’ in Chinese. You can use either …三十 or …半.

If the number of minutes is more than 10 then the character 分 after the number of minutes can be omitted. For example, to say 05:20, you can say either 五点二十 or 五点二十分.

The Chinese for two when counting is 二, but when saying ‘two o’clock’ or being asked ‘how many’ you should use 两 **liǎng**.

New hanzi

两	liǎng	two

 Character building

两 一 丆 币 丙 丙 两 两

Now let's do some exercises.

Exercise 1

Look at the pictures below and write out the time shown in each.

Example:

 十一点十五

1)

2)

. . . .

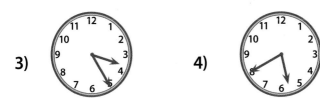

3)

4)

. . . .

5)

. . . .

Exercise 2

Write the following pinyin sentences in characters. Say the Chinese out loud as you do this.

What time is it?

1) sān diǎn shí liù (fēn) . . . .

2) wǔ diǎn sì shí sān (fēn) . . . .

3) shí èr diǎn sì shí bā (fēn) . . . .

4) qī diǎn wǔ shí jiǔ (fēn) . . . .

5) jiǔ diǎn bàn . . . .

Lesson 10

Exercise 3

Circle the correct Chinese translation and write it out.
How much time have you spent?

1) Two hours. （ 一小时， 二小时， 两小时 ）

· ·

2) Three hours and forty minutes. （ 三小时四十分， 三小时四分， 三小时十四分 ）

· ·

3) Two and a half hours. （ 两小时三十分， 二小时三十分， 两小时二十分 ）

· ·

4) Four and a half hours. （ 四小时三十分， 四小时二十分， 四小时二十五分 ）

· ·

Exercise 4

Fill in the empty boxes to form a complete character.

1) 分 ☐ ☐ ☐ ☐

2) 半 ☐ ☐ ☐ ☐

3) 点 ☐ ☐ ☐ ☐ ☐ ☐
☐ ☐

Lesson 11 ~ *am and pm*

*N*ow *we're going to learn how to say am and pm.*

This will involve a couple of characters that we have already learned.
Can you identify them in the following list?

Puzzle

早上	zǎo shàng	early morning
上午	shàng wǔ	morning
中午	zhōng wǔ	noon
下午	xià wǔ	afternoon
晚上	wǎn shàng	evening

The answers are at the back of the book.

Character building

早 | 丨 | 冂 | 冃 | 日 | 旦 | 早 |

上　丨　卜　上

午　丿　𠂉　𠂉　午

中　丨　冂　口　中

下　一　丁　下

晚　丨　冂　日　日　日′　日″　日″　日甶

日免　日免　晚

Let's do some exercises to get familiar with these characters.

Exercise 1

Circle the odd man out.

1) 上午　　中午　　下牛

2) 上午　　中午　　卜午

3) 上午　　申午　　下午

4) 上午　　中午　　下干

5) 土午　　下午　　中午

Exercise 2

Write out the times below in Chinese characters. Say your answers out loud. For example:

7:00 am　早上七点　zǎo shàng qī diǎn

> You say am/pm before you say the time.

1) 6:00 am　...

2) 12:00 am　...

3) 5:25 pm　...

4) 3:40 pm　...

5) 4:30 pm　...

6) 8.00 pm　...

Exercise 3

Write the following pinyin in characters. Remember to say your answers out loud.

What time is it?

1) xià wǔ sān diǎn shí liù fēn

15 : 16

....

2) xià wǔ wǔ diǎn sì shí sān fēn

17 : 43

....

3) zhōng wǔ shí èr diǎn shí fēn

12 : 10

....

4) zǎo shàng qī diǎn wǔ shí jiǔ fēn

07 : 59

....

5) shàng wǔ jiǔ diǎn bàn

09 : 30

....

Lesson 11

Lesson 12 ~ *Days of the week*

*I*n this lesson, we are going to learn the characters for the days of the week. For Monday to Saturday you will need to know Chinese numbers plus 星 期 xīng qī or 周 zhōu.

星	xīng	star
期	qī	period
周	zhōu	week

character building

星

丨	冂	冃	日	尸	尸	彐

星	星

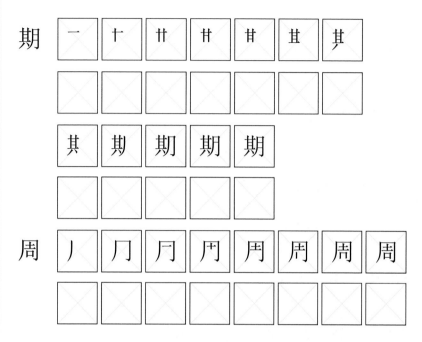

The days are:

星 期 一	xīng qī yī	Monday
星 期 二	xīng qī èr	Tuesday
星 期 三	xīng qī sān	Wednesday
星 期 四	xīng qī sì	Thursday
星 期 五	xīng qī wǔ	Friday
星 期 六	xīng qī liù	Saturday

or you can say:

周 一	zhōu yī	Monday
周 二	zhōu èr	Tuesday
周 三	zhōu sān	Wednesday
周 四	zhōu sì	Thursday
周 五	zhōu wǔ	Friday
周 六	zhōu liù	Saturday

Sunday is different.

星 期 天	xīng qī tiān	Sunday
周 日	zhōu rì	Sunday

New hanzi

天	tiān	day; sky
日	rì	day

Character building

天	一	二	于	天

日	丨	冂	日	日

Exercise 1

Circle the odd man out.

1) 天　日　夫　周

2) 日　四　天　周

3) 日　天　周　用

4) 天　日　田　周

Exercise 2

These columns have got jumbled up. Use the characters you have learned above to put the correct Chinese against the English. Write the characters down.

1) Monday . . . . 周六

2) Tuesday . . . . 星期四

3) Wednesday . . . . 星期日

4) Thursday . . . . 周五

5) Friday . . . . 周一

6) Saturday . . . . 周三

7) Sunday . . . . 星期二

Exercise 3

Write the pinyin in characters. Say your answers out loud.

1) zhōu rì shàng wǔ . . . .

2) zhōu sì zhōng wǔ . . . .

3) zhōu liù xià wǔ . . . .

4) zhōu èr xià wǔ yī diǎn bàn

. . . .

5) zhōu wǔ xià wǔ sì diǎn sì shí

. . . .

6) zhōu rì zhōng wǔ shí èr diǎn

. . . .

Lesson 12

Lesson 13 ~ *People*

In this lesson we are going to learn some basic characters for people.

人	rén	person
男	nán	male
女	nǚ	female

男人 nán rén man   女人 nǚ rén woman

老人 lǎo rén old person   孩子 hái zi child

Character building

人 ｜ 丿 ｜ 人 ｜

男 ｜ 丨 ｜ 冂 ｜ 冃 ｜ 用 ｜ 田 ｜ 罗 ｜ 男 ｜

女 ｜ 一 ｜ 乚 ｜ 女 ｜

老 ｜ 一 ｜ 十 ｜ 土 ｜ 耂 ｜ 老 ｜ 老 ｜

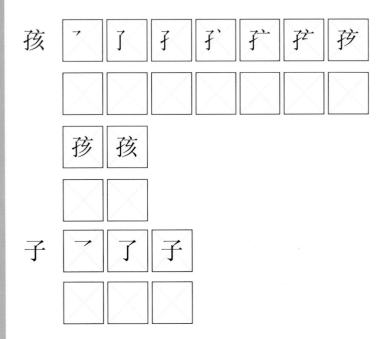

Learning Tips

We can use some of the above characters to make word combinations.

男	孩子	男孩子	*or*	男孩	
		nán hái zi	*or*	nán hái	boy(s)
女	孩子	女孩子	*or*	女孩	
		nǚ hái zi	*or*	nǚ hái	girl(s)

Now let's do some exercises. In some of these you will need to use the character 个 gè. *This is a measure word or count word used before nouns in combination with a number, when saying, for example, 3 men or 5 women.*

 *Character building*

个 gè

ノ	人	个

Exercise 1

Circle the odd man out.

1) 男　女　力　老

2) 男　女　田　老

3) 孩　子　男　安

4) 人　入　男　女

5) 孩　子　了　女

6) 人　女　子　好

Exercise 2

These captions have got jumbled up. Use the words you have learned above to rearrange them correctly.

1)   **2)**   **3)**   **4)**

女人   孩子   男人   老人

. . . .

Exercise 3

Translate the following sentences into characters. Write down the answers and say them out loud.

Example: three children 三个孩子 sān ge hái zi

1) one old person   . . . .

2) ten women   . . . .

3) one hundred and

thirty seven people   . . . .

4) forty men   . . . .

5) fifteen children   . . . .

Exercise 4

Fill in the empty stroke sequence boxes to form a complete character. In two cases part of the character has already been written for you.

1) 女

2) 男 田

3) 老 土

4) 子

5) 个

Lesson 14 ~ *Families*

*I*n this lesson we are going to learn some characters to describe a family.

祖	父	zǔ fù	grandfather
祖	母	zǔ mǔ	grandmother
父	亲	fù qīn	father
母	亲	mǔ qīn	mother
儿	子	ér zi	son
女	儿	nǚ ér	daughter
孙	子	sūn zi	grandson
孙	女	sūn nǚ	granddaughter

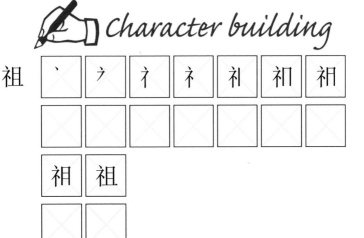

Character building

祖	丶	礻	礻	礻	礻	衵	袒

袒	祖

父 | ノ | 八 | 分 | 父

母 |乚 | 口 | 母 | 母 | 母

亲 | 丶 | 亠 | 六 | 立 | 辛 | 辛 | 辛

辛 | 亲

儿 | ノ | 儿

孙 | フ | 了 | 子 | 孑 | 孙 | 孙

These characters can be used to form some fixed combinations. For example:

父母	parents
子女	children
父子	father and son
父女	father and daughter
母子	mother and son
母女	mother and daughter

Now it's time to do some exercises.

Exercise 1

These captions have got jumbled up. Use the words you have learned above to rearrange them correctly.

1)	2)	3)	4)
母亲	孙女	祖母	祖父
. . . . .	. . . . .	. . . . .	. . . . .

Exercise 2

Circle the odd man out.

1) 祖 母 孙 租

2) 父 母 爻 儿

3) 祖 孙 几 父

4) 孙 了 子 祖

Exercise 3

Here are two important new Chinese characters which
you are going to need for the rest of this lesson:

是	shì	to be; is, are
的	de	of; used after an adjective coming before a noun

character building

是 | 丨 | 冂 | 円 | 日 | 旦 | 早 | 昰 |

| | | | | |

| 昰 | 是 |

| |

的 | ⼃ | ⼻ | 冇 | 白 | 白 | 白 | 的 | 的 |

| | | | | | | |

Here are some family relationships:

Jack is Hilda's son.

Tom is Jane's father.

George is Jimmy's grandfather.

Sheila is Peter's grandmother.

Now complete the following sentences. Write down the answers and say them out loud. Use English for the English names.

1) George 是 Jimmy 的 . . . . 。

2) Sheila 是 Peter 的 . . . . 。

3) Jack 是 Hilda 的 . . . . 。

4) Jimmy 是 George 的 . . . . 。

5) Hilda 是 Jack 的 . . . . 。

6) Jane 是 Tom 的 . . . . 。

Puzzle

Here's a special day that families celebrate.

母 亲 节

Can you puzzle out what it's called in English?

Lesson 14

Lesson 15 ~ *Yesterday, today and tomorrow*

*I*n this lesson, we are going to learn the characters for
some common time-related words: yesterday, today,
tomorrow and the day after tomorrow.

昨 天	zuó tiān	yesterday
今 天	jīn tiān	today
明 天	míng tiān	tomorrow
后 天	hòu tiān	the day after tomorrow

Character building

昨 zuó | 丨 | 冂 | 日 | 日 | 日′ | 日⺁ | 昨 |

| | | | | | |

| 昨 | 昨 |

| |

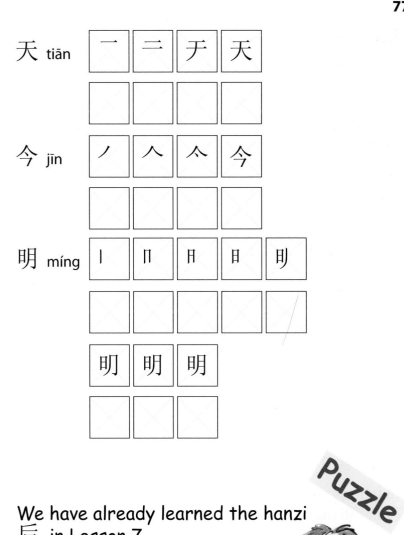

We have already learned the hanzi
后 in Lesson 7.

Can you remember what it
meant then?

Puzzle

Exercise 1

Look at this list of days and complete each question in hanzi.

周一
周二
周三 ← 今天
周四
周五
周六
周日

1) 今天是… . . . .

2) 昨天是… . . . .

3) 明天是… . . . .

4) 后天是… . . . .

Exercise 2

Study the example and then translate the following bits of English into characters. Write down the answers and say them out loud.

Example: Today is Friday. 今 天 是 周 五 。 Jīn tiān shì zhōu wǔ.

1) two o'clock this afternoon

. . . .

2) 8 o'clock yesterday morning

. . . .

3) Tomorrow is Wednesday.

. . . .

4) The day after tomorrow is Sunday.

. . . .

5) 2 o'clock on Saturday afternoon

. . . .

6) 10:40 on Tuesday morning

. . . .

Lesson 16 ~ *Months, years and dates*

In this lesson we are going to learn the characters for months and years.

Use this with days but not months.

月	yuè	month
年	nián	year
下	xià	next
去 年	qù nián	last year
今 年	jīn nián	this year
明 年	míng nián	next year

Character building

月	丿	刀	月	月

年	丿	⺊	⺦	⺫	乍	年

去	一	十	土	去	去

To say a month in Chinese just put its number (1-12) in front of 月.

To say a date in Chinese the sequence is: year/month/day.

For example, 7th July 2008 in Chinese is: 2008年7月7日 or 二零零八年七月七日.

Chinese uses Arabic numbers as well as Chinese characters.

For 'last December' or 'next May' Chinese says 'last year December' or 'next year May'.

New hanzi

有	yǒu	have, has, have got; there is; there are

Exercise 1

Complete the following Chinese sentences using the characters you have learned. Say the answers out loud.

1) 一年有 ...... 个月

2) 一小时有 ...... 分

3) 半小时有 ...... 分

4) 一天有 ...... 个小时

Exercise 2

Study this example and then translate the following sentences into characters. Say your answers out loud.

Example: September 1st 1993 一九九三年九月一日
yī jiǔ jiǔ sān nián jiǔ yuè yī rì

1) July 5th 1998 ....

2) last December ....

3) next January ....

4) next Monday ....

Lesson 16

5) September 18th this year

· ·

6) April 13th last year

· ·

Exercise 3

Read the following paragraph. Underline the correct answer to each of the Chinese questions below and say the answer out loud.

Today is Friday, 11th of May. Jane got up at 7 o'clock in the morning. She went to school at 7:30 and arrived there at 8:10, which was ten minutes late. She went to the cinema after school at 3:45 in the afternoon. Tomorrow is her birthday and there is a party at her home at 4 o'clock in the afternoon. Her grandmother will come from London to go to the party.

Example:　今天是⋯（ 星期四， <u>星期五</u>，星期六， 星期天 ） xīng qī wǔ

1) 昨天是⋯

（ 五月九日， 五月十日， 五月十一日，五月十二日 ）

2) 明天是⋯

（ 五月十一日， 五月十二日， 五月十三日， 五月十四日 ）

3) 后天是…

（ 周五， 周六， 周日， 周一 ）

4) Jane got up at …

（ 下午四点， 上午六点， 下午七点，
早上七点 ）

5) Jane arrived at school at…

（ 上午八点， 上午九点， 上午十点，
早上八点十分 ）

6) Jane should have got to school at…

（ 早上八点， 上午九点， 上午八点十分，
上午十点 ）

7) Jane went to see the film at…

（ 下午三点十分， 上午三点十五，
上午三点四十， 下午三点四十五 ）

8) Jane's birthday is on…

（ 周三， 周四， 周五， 周六 ）

9) Jane's birthday party is at…

（ 下午四点十分， 上午四点十五，
上午四点， 下午四点 ）

10) What date is Jane's birthday?

（ 五月十日， 五月十一日， 五月十二日，
五月十三日 ）

11) Who will come from London to celebrate Jane's birthday?

（Jane 的祖父，　Jane 的祖母，

Jane 的父亲，　Jane 的母亲 ）

Lesson 17 ~ *Family members*

*I*n this lesson we will start with some characters for family members. These are more colloquial words than the ones in Lesson 14.

爸 爸 bà ba dad

妈 妈 mā ma mum

爷 爷 yé ye grandpa

奶 奶 nǎi nai grandma

Do you recognise anything in the hanzi for 'dad'? Check back on page 70.

Character building

爸	⼂	⼋	⼉	父	兮	爷	爸	爸

妈	一	七	女	奵	妈	妈

爷	⼂	⼋	⼉	父	兮	爷

奶	一	七	女	奶	奶

Now let's do some exercises.

Exercise 1

Circle the odd man out.

1) 爸 妈 好 爷   **3)** 爷 妈 奶 斧

2) 妈 笆 爷 奶   **4)** 爸 爷 乃 妈

Exercise 2

These captions have got jumbled up. Use the hanzi you have learned above to rearrange them correctly.

1)   **2)**   **3)**   **4)**

爷爷   奶奶   妈妈   爸爸

· · · · ·   · · · · ·   · · · · ·   · · · · ·

Exercise 3

Read these sentences.

Tom is Jane's dad.

Hilda is Jack's mum.

George is Jimmy's grandpa.

Sheila is Peter's grandma.

Now complete the following sentences, writing your answers down and saying them out loud.

1) George 是 Jimmy 的 . . . . 。

2) Tom 是 Jane 的 . . . . 。

3) Sheila 是 Peter 的 . . . . 。

4) Hilda 是 Jack 的 . . . . 。

Exercise 4

Fill in the empty stroke sequence boxes to complete the character which has been started in the second box.

1) 爸 | 父 | | | |

2) 妈 | 女 | | |

3) 爷 | 父 | |

4) 奶 | 女 | |

Lesson 18 ~ *More family members*

In this lesson we are going to learn some more hanzi for family members.

哥哥 gē ge
older brother

姐姐 jiě jie
older sister

弟弟 dì di
younger brother

妹妹 mèi mei
younger sister

Character building

哥 | 一 | 丁 | 丌 | 可 | 可 | 可 | 哥 | 哥

哥 | 哥

姐 | 一 | 乚 | 女 | 刘 | 如 | 姐 | 姐 | 姐

弟 | 丶 | 丷 | 丷 | 当 | 弟 | 弟

妹 | 一 | 乚 | 女 | 女 | 妒 | 奸 | 妹 | 妹

Now let's do some exercises.

Exercise 1

Circle the odd man out.

1) 哥　歌　弟　妹

2) 姐　如　哥　妹

3) 妹　哥　姐　第

4) 姐　弟　哥　昧

Exercise 2

These captions have got jumbled up. Use the hanzi you have learned above to rearrange them correctly.

1)　　　　　2)　　　　　3)　　　　　4)

姐姐　　　妹妹　　　哥哥　　　弟弟

.....　　　.....　　　.....　　　.....

Exercise 3

Read the following sentences.

Bob is Mandy's older brother.　　Amy is Bob's older sister.

Now complete the following sentences, writing your answers down and saying them out loud.

1) Mandy 是 Bob 的 . . . . 。

2) Bob 是 Mandy 的 . . . . 。

3) Amy 是 Bob 的 . . . . 。

4) Bob 是 Amy 的 . . . . 。

Lesson 19 ~ *Nature*

*I*n this lesson we are going to learn some characters for talking about nature.

云 yún cloud

月 yuè moon

光 guāng light

山 shān mountain

风 fēng wind

雨 yǔ rain

Which of these characters has already been introduced in an earlier lesson with a different meaning? Answer on page 94

Answer on page 94

Lesson 19

Character building

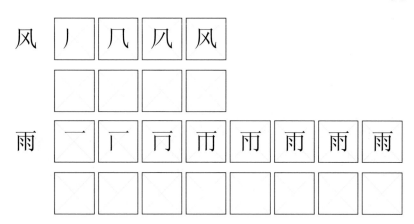

Learning Tips

We can use these hanzi to form some common word combinations.

月 + 光　月光　　moonlight
风 + 光　风光　　scenery

Exercise 1

Circle the odd man out.

1) 云　月　耳　山　　4) 凤　雨　山　月

2) 月　云　用　光　　5) 风　需　云　山

3) 山　月　元　云

Exercise 2

These captions have got jumbled up. Use the words you have learned above to rearrange them correctly.

1)   **2)**   **3)**   **4)**

雨   月   山   云

. . . .

> 月 also means month

Exercise 3

Fill in the empty stroke sequence boxes to form a complete character.

1) 风

2) 云

3) 山

4) 光

5) 月

Lesson 20 ~ *More about nature*

L et's learn some more basic characters to describe nature.

木 mù wood

土 tǔ earth; land

火 huǒ fire

水 shuǐ water

冰 bīng ice

河 hé river

Character building

木 | 一 | 十 | 才 | 木

土 | 一 | 十 | 土

火 | 丿 | 丷 | 火 | 火

水 | 亅 | 水 | 水 | 水

冰 | 丶 | 冫 | 冮 | 冴 | 冰 | 冰

河 | ` | ⸜ | 氵 | 氵 | 汀 | 汈 | 河 | 河

Here are a couple of interesting character formations. Try to figure out the meanings first and then check your answers against the new hanzi list.

Puzzle

木 + 木 = 林

木 + 木 + 木 = 森

Let's do some exercises.

Exercise 1

Circle the odd man out.

1) 土 王 水 木

2) 火 冰 本 水

3) 木 土 何 冰

4) 水 永 冰 火

5) 伙 木 土 河

6) 木 士 水 火

New hanzi

林	lín	woods
森	sēn	forest
森 林	sēn lín	dense forest

Exercise 2

These captions have got jumbled up. Use the words you have learned above to rearrange them correctly.

1) 木 . . . . . .   2) 土 . . . . . .

3) 河 . . . . . .   4) 火 . . . . . .

Exercise 3

Fill in the empty stroke sequence boxes to form a complete character.

1) 水 □□□□

2) 土 □□□

3) 火 □□□□

4) 木 □□□

5) 冰 □□□□□□

Exercise 4

Write out the character which has the highest number of strokes in each of these groups. Say this character out loud.

1) 山 土 火 光 ....

2) 水 手 头 舌 ....

3) 冰 男 木 妈 ....

4) 子 个 月 上 ....

5) 河 爸 姐 哥 ....

Lesson 20

Quiz

Do you remember the characters learned in Block 1? If you need to, use the glossaries at the back of the book to do this quiz.

1) 二十一 Is this the Chinese for
   a) 12; **b)** 21; **c)** 11?

2) 八十 Is this the Chinese for
   a) 18; **b)** 60; **c)** 80?

3) Chinese has a single character for 10,000. True or false?

4) 星期四 Which day of the week is this?

5) 十三减七等于六 True or false?

6) Most people eat breakfast around 十二点. True or false?

7) Most people keep their TV 在 table 下. True or false?

8) 三 One stroke is missing to complete the Chinese for hand. Write the full character.

9) Hannah is 16 and her sister Josie is 9. Is Josie Hannah's 姐姐 **jiě jie** or 妹妹 **mèi mei**?

10) What happens if you put 水 on 火?

Lesson 1 ~ *Personal pronouns*

In this lesson we are going to learn some characters for personal pronouns.

我	wǒ	I; me
你	nǐ	you *(singular)*
他	tā	he; him
她	tā	she; her
它	tā	it

Can you recognize the first part of this character? Check Block 1 Lesson 13.

character building

我 | 一 | 二 | 于 | 于 | 我 | 我 | 我

你 | ノ | 亻 | 亻 | 伫 | 你 | 你 | 你

Lesson 1

Do you remember we learned the characters 在 and 边 in Block 1 Lesson 5 and 是 in Block 1 Lesson 14? Why not check them now? We are going to use them as well as the new characters to do some exercises.

Exercise 1

Circle the odd man out.

1) 你 我 地 她

2) 它 她 找 他

3) 我 奶 他 它

4) 宅 他 你 她

Exercise 2

These English words have got jumbled up. Write the correct ones under each Chinese character.

1)	**2)**	**3)**	**4)**	**5)**
他	我	她	它	你
it	you	he	I	she

. . . . .　. . . . .　. . . . .　. . . . .　. . . . .

Exercise 3

Translate the following sentences into Chinese characters. Write down the answers and say them out loud.

Example: She is Jane. 她是Jane. Tā shì Jane.

1) It is inside. . . . .

2) You are the older brother. . . . .

3) I am the younger sister. . . . .

4) She is the older sister. . . . .

5) I'm the younger brother. . . . .

6) He is a dad. . . . .

7) She is a mum. . . . .

8) He's a grandpa. . . . .

9) She's a grandma. . . . .

Lesson 2 ~ *Some common verbs*

*I*n this lesson we are going to learn some characters expressing actions.

来	lái	to come; to arrive
去	qù	to go
回	huí	to return; to go back
走	zǒu	to walk; to leave; to move
坐	zuò	to sit
做	zuò	to do; to make

character building

来	一	丶	丷	平	平	来	来

去	一	十	土	去	去

回	丨	冂	冂	同	同	回

走	一	十	土	丰	丰	走	走

坐	丿	人	从	从	丛	坐	坐

做	丿	亻	仁	什	仕	估	估	做

做	做	做

You can make word combinations using these characters, combinations which are more often used in spoken Chinese than the single characters. Read the following and say each compound out loud.

来回 round trip   回去 to go back

回来 to come back   走回去 to walk back

坐下 to sit down

In Chinese we use the character 了 le to indicate a completed action.

For example: She walked away. 她走了。

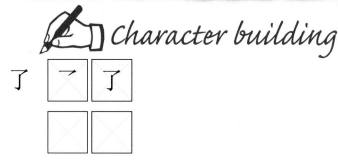

Character building

了 | マ | 了

Let's do some exercises.

Exercise 1

Circle the odd man out.

1) 去 走 未 回   4) 故 来 坐 走

2) 坐 座 去 做   5) 坐 去 徒 做

3) 回 水 去 做

Exercise 2

These English words have got jumbled up. Use the words you have learned above to match them up correctly.

1)	2)	3)	4)	5)	6)
回	来	去	做	走	坐
to sit	to walk	to return	to come	to go	to do

. . . .

Exercise 3

Choose the correct answer from the three possibilities.

For example
She walked away.
（她走了，他来了，她去了） 她走了。

1) Dad went back. （妈妈回来了，爸爸回去了，
   爸爸回来了） . . . .

2) He sat down. （她坐下了，他坐下了，
   他走了） . . . .

3) She left yesterday. （他昨天来了，
   她昨天走了，她今天走了）

. . . .

Lesson 2

4) I arrived at 8:40 this morning. （我今天上午八点
四十来了, 你今天下午八点四十来了,
你今天上午八点四十来了）

. . . .

5) Mum came back yesterday afternoon.

（妈妈昨天下午回去了, 妈妈昨天上午回
来了, 妈妈昨天下午回来了）

. . . .

Lesson 3 ~ *Some more verbs*

*I*n this lesson we are going to learn another series of
*characters expressing actions. Let's have a look at the
new characters listed below.*

看	kàn	to look at; to see; to watch
写	xiě	to write
笑	xiào	to laugh
哭	kū	to cry
说	shuō	to talk; to speak; to say
问	wèn	to ask; to query

Lesson 3

Character building

看 | 一 | 二 | 三 | 手 | 乔 | 乔 | 看

看 | 看

写 | ﹑ | 宀 | 写 | 写 | 写

笑 | ノ | ⺮ | ⺮ | ⺮ | 竹 | 竹 | 竺 | 竺

竿 | 笑

哭 | 丨 | 冂 | 口 | 叩 | 叩 | 吅 | 哭 | 哭

哭 | 哭

说 | 丶 | 讠 | 讠 | 讠 | 讠 | 讶 | 说

讶 | 说

问 | 丶 | 冂 | 门 | 问 | 问 | 问

Exercise 1

Circle the odd man out.

1) 写　着　说　笑　　　　**4)** 写　说　看　笋

2) 哭　军　问　看　　　　**5)** 说　哭　间　看

3) 悦　笑　看　写

Exercise 2

These hanzi have got jumbled up. Use the words you have learned above to match them up with the English.

1)	**2)**	**3)**	**4)**	**5)**	**6)**
to look at	to laugh	to cry	to say	to write	to ask
哭	说	写	笑	问	看

. . . . .　　. . . . .　　. . . . .　　. . . . .　　. . . . .　　. . . . .

Exercise 3

Choose the correct answer from the three possibilities.

For example
She cried.
（他笑了，她哭了，她笑了）　　她哭了。

1) The younger sister cried. （妹妹哭了，妹妹笑了，

妹妹走了）　　. . . . .

2) I did it yesterday.　　（我昨天来了，

我昨天做了，我昨天问了）. . . . .

3) I watched it the day before yesterday.
（我前天看了，他前天看了，她前天写了）

. . . .

4) He wrote it.　　（你写了，我写了，他写了）

. . . .

Chinese often omits 'it'.

Lesson 4

Lesson 4 ~ *Word combinations*

*I*n this lesson we are going to learn some word combinations using the action words from Lesson 3. Take a few minutes first to go over those characters in Lessons 2 and 3 of Block 2, and then study the following compounds.

看 + 书 shū book　　　　看书 to read (a book)

看 + 见 jiàn to see, to meet　　看见 to see

写 + 书 shū book　　　　写书 to write a book

写 + 字 zì word; character   写字 to write (Chinese)

说 + 话 huà speech; language; conversation   说话 to speak; to talk

回 + 家 jiā home   回家 to go home

做 + 事 shì thing; matter   做事 to work

Character building

书 | ㇕ | 乛 | 书 | 书

见 | ㇑ | 冂 | 贝 | 见

字 | 丶 | 丷 | 宀 | 宁 | 宁 | 字

话 ｜ ` ｜ 讠 ｜ 讠 ｜ 讠 ｜ 讦 ｜ 许 ｜ 话 ｜ 话

家 ｜ ` ｜ 丶 ｜ 宀 ｜ 宀 ｜ 宇 ｜ 宁 ｜ 豸

家 ｜ 家 ｜ 家

事 ｜ 一 ｜ 一 ｜ 一 ｜ 一 ｜ 弖 ｜ 弖 ｜ 弖 ｜ 事

In Chinese we use the character 在 zài to indicate a continuous tense.

For example: She is reading a book. 她在看书。

Exercise 1

These English words have got jumbled up. Use the words you have just learned to match up English and Chinese.

1)	2)	3)	4)	5)	6)
回家	看书	做事	写字	写书	说话
to work	to write a book	to go home	to talk	to read a book	to write

. . . .

Exercise 2

Choose the correct answer from the three possibilities.

For example

She's reading a book. （她在写字, 她在看书, 他在写字） 她在看书。

1) I'm writing. （我在看书, 我在写字, 我在写书） . . . .

2) Dad's reading. （爸爸在看书, 爸爸在写字, 爸爸在写书） . . . .

3) Mum is talking. （妈妈说话了, 妈妈在说话, 妈妈要说话） . . . .

Lesson 4

4) Grandpa is writing a book. （爷爷在看书，

爷爷在写书，爷爷写书了） . . . .

5) She has gone home. （我回家了, 他回家了,

她回家了） . . . .

6) Grandma is meeting me at 3pm tomorrow.

（奶奶明天下午三点见我， 奶奶明天早

上三点见我， 奶奶明天下午四点见我）

. . . .

7) I saw she was reading. （我看见他在看书,

我看见她看书, 我看见她在看书）

. . . .

Lesson 5 ~ *Some question words*

*I*n this lesson we are going to learn some key question words.

什么？	shén me?	what?
什么时候？	shén me shí hòu?	when?
为什么？	wèi shén me?	why?
谁？	shéi?	who?

character building

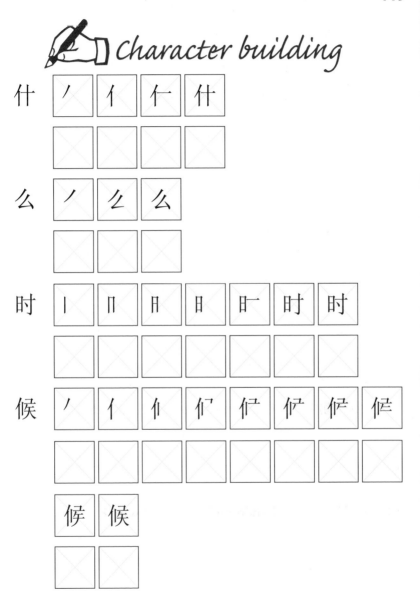

什　｜丿｜亻｜仁｜什｜
　　｜　｜　｜　｜

么　｜丿｜厶｜么｜
　　｜　｜　｜

时　｜丨｜冂｜日｜日｜旷｜时｜时｜
　　｜　｜　｜　｜　｜　｜

候　｜丿｜亻｜亻｜亻'｜俨｜俨｜俟｜候｜
　　｜　｜　｜　｜　｜　｜　｜

　　｜侯｜候｜
　　｜　｜

为 ｜ `丶` ｜ `勹` ｜ `为` ｜ `为`

谁 ｜ `丶` ｜ `讠` ｜ `讠` ｜ `讠` ｜ `讠` ｜ `讠` ｜ `讠` ｜ `诈`

谁 ｜ `诈` ｜ `谁`

Chinese word order is sometimes different to English. 他做什么? What is he doing?

Now let's do some exercises.

Exercise 1

Circle the characters that we have just learned.

1) 仕么　　什公　　什么

2) 什公时侯　什么时侯　什么时候

3) 为什公　　为什么　　力什么

4) 淮　　惟　　谁

Exercise 2

These English words have got jumbled up. Can you match them up correctly with the hanzi?

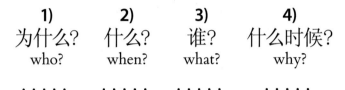

1)	**2)**	**3)**	**4)**
为什么?	什么?	谁?	什么时候?
who?	when?	what?	why?

. . . . .　　. . . . .　　. . . . .　　. . . . .

Exercise 3

Choose the correct answer from the three possibilities. Say the correct answer out loud.

Example
Who is reading a book?

（谁在写字?，谁在看书?，谁在写字?）

谁在看书? Shéi zài kàn shū?

1) When did he go home yesterday?

（他昨天为什么回家?, 她昨天什么时候回家?, 他昨天什么时候回家了?）

. . . .

2) Why is she crying? （她什么时候哭了?, 他为什么在笑?, 她为什么在哭?）

. . . .

Lesson 5

3) What did mum say? （妈妈什么时候说了?，妈妈说什么了?，妈妈为什么说?）

· ·

4) Who is talking? （谁在说话?，谁在看书?，谁在做事?）

· ·

5) Who did you ask? （你问谁了?, 谁问你了?, 谁说你了?）

· ·

6) What are you watching? （他在看什么?她在看什么?，你在看什么?）

· ·

Exercise 4

Make these into complete questions by choosing the correct question word from the text in brackets. Say the Chinese out loud when you do this.

Example:

他在看…? （为什么，什么，什么时候）
``什么 Tā zài kàn shén me?

1) 你…回家了? （什么时候, 什么, 谁）

· ·

2) 你昨天下午做…了？　（为什么, 什么, 谁）

. . . .

3) 她在做…？　（什么, 为什么, 什么时候）

. . . .

4) …在说话？　（什么, 谁, 什么时候）

. . . .

Exercise 5

Supply the missing character to complete these dialogues.

1)

他是……？

他是我爷爷。

2)

……是谁？

她是我妹妹。

3)

他是谁？

他是……。

Lesson 6 ~ *Some function words*

*I*n this lesson we are going to learn a group of key function words.

从	cóng	from
和	hé	and
正 在	zhèng zài	*used to indicate continuous action*
已 经	yǐ jīng	already

You can use either 在 or 正在 with the same meaning.

To express somebody 'comes from...' we need to say 从...来. For example:

他从中国来。 He comes from China.

Here are the characters for some names which you'll need later on in the exercises.

中国	Zhōng guó	China
美国	Měi guó	America
英国	Yīng guó	Britain
北京	Běijīng	Beijing
上海	Shànghǎi	Shanghai

Lesson 6

Exercise 1

Identify the characters that we have just learned from the three options in brackets and write them down.

1) （丛, 从, 人） . . . .

2) （禾, 种, 和） . . . .

3) （正左, 止在, 正在） . . . .

4) （己经, 巳经, 已经） . . . .

Exercise 2

These English words have got jumbled up. Use the words you have learned above to match them up correctly.

| **1)**
已经
from | **2)**
正在
and | **3)**
和
already | **4)**
从
continuous
tense indicator |

. . . .

Exercise 3

Identify the Chinese which correctly translates each of these bits of English. Write it in the space provided and say the Chinese out loud.

1) Him and her. （她和他, 他和她, 他和它）

. . . .

2) You and me. （你和他，你和她，你和我）

· ·

3) Mum and Dad. （妈妈和姐姐，妈妈和爸爸，爸爸和妈妈）

· ·

4) He is from Britain. （他从英国来，他从美国来，他从中国来）

· ·

5) I'm from Shanghai. （我从北京来，我从上海来，他从上海来）

· ·

6) She's reading. （她正在看书，他正在看书，她正在看）

· ·

7) He has already gone. （她走了，他要走，他已经走了）

· ·

8) I have already done it. （你做了，我做了，我已经做了）

· ·

Lesson 6

Lesson 7 ~ *Personal pronouns in the plural*

*I*n this lesson we are going to learn an important plural marker for pronouns.

们	men	*plural marker for pronouns*

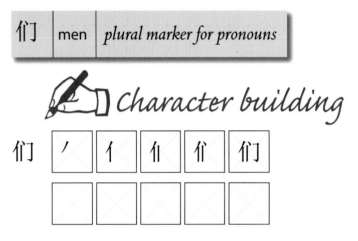

character building

们	ノ	亻	仆	伩	们

Now let's have a look at the plural pronouns in Chinese.

我们	wǒ men	we; us
你们	nǐ men	you *(plural)*
他们	tā men	they; them
她们	tā men	they; them *(feminine only)*
它们	tā men	they; them *(for inanimate objects)*

Exercise 1

These English words have got jumbled up. Use the words you have learned above to match them up correctly.

1)	2)	3)	4)
我们	她们	他们	你们
they	you	us	they (*feminine*)

. . . .

Exercise 2

Identify the Chinese which correctly translates each of these bits of English. Write it in the space provided and say the Chinese out loud.

1) They have already gone. （他们已经来了，我们已经走了，他们已经走了）

. . . .

2) We're talking. （他们正在说话，我们正在说话，我正在说话）

. . . .

3) Why are you laughing? （你们为什么在笑？，他们为什么在笑？，她们为什么在笑？）

. . . .

Lesson 7

4) They have already gone *(masculine)*.

（我们已经走了，她们已经来了，

他们已经走了）

. . . .

5) They're crying *(feminine)*. （她们在哭，

我们在哭，它们哭了）

. . . .

Lesson 8 ~ *Possessives*

*I*n this lesson we are going to learn to work with a key word for forming possessives, the hanzi 的 which was introduced back in Block One Lesson 14.

Now have a look at the following possessives.

我 的	wǒ de	my; mine
你 的	nǐ de	your; yours
他 的	tā de	his
她 的	tā de	her; hers
它 的	tā de	its

我 们 的	wǒ men de	our; ours
你 们 的	nǐ men de	your; yours
他 们 的	tā men de	their; theirs *(masculine)*
她 们 的	tā men de	their; theirs *(feminine)*
它 们 的	tā men de	their; theirs *(inanimate)*

Exercise 1

Hanzi and English are jumbled up. Write the correct English under each hanzi. Say the Chinese out loud.

1)	2)	3)	4)	5)
它的	他们的	你的	我们的	她的
her	ours	its	their	your

. . . . .　. . . . .　. . . . .　. . . . .　. . . . .

Exercise 2

Identify the Chinese which correctly translates each of these bits of English. Write it in the space provided and say the Chinese out loud.

1) He is my grandpa.　（他是我们的爷爷，

他是我的爷爷，　他是你的爷爷）

. . . .

2) She is his elder sister. （她是她的姐姐，

他是她的姐姐，她是他的姐姐）

. . . .

3) They are my mum and dad.

（他是我的妈妈和爸爸，她们是我的妈

妈和爸爸，他们是我的妈妈和爸爸）

. . . .

4) It is yours. （它是你的，它们是你的，

它是他们的）

. . . .

5) His younger brother is reading a book.

（她的弟弟正在看书，他的弟弟正在看书,

他们的弟弟正在看书）

. . . .

Exercise 3

Translate the following sentences into English.

1) 我的手。. . . . .

2) 我们的妹妹们。. . . . .

3) 她的头发。. . . . .

4) 他们的父母。. . . . .

5) 你们的子女。. . . . .

Lesson 9 ~ *Key demonstrative pronouns*

In this lesson we are going to learn some important characters for referring to people and things.

这		zhè	this
这	个	zhè ge	this (one)
这	些	zhè xiē	these
那		nà	that
那	个	nà ge	that (one)
那	些	nà xiē	those
这	里	zhè lǐ	here
那	里	nà lǐ	there

Character building

这 | 、 | 一 | 亠 | 文 | 文 | 讠 | 这

些 | ㅣ | ㅏ | � | 止 | 此 | 此 | 些 | 些

里 | ㅣ | 冂 | 冃 | 日 | 甲 | 甲 | 里

那 | 乛 | 彐 | 彐 | 刅 | 刅 | 那′ | 那

Now let's do some exercises (in combination with
the character 是 where necessary).

Exercise 1

Hanzi and pinyin have got jumbled up. Can you write
the correct pinyin for each hanzi?

1)	2)	3)	4)	5)	6)
那些	这里	这些	这个	那里	这
zhè ge	nà lǐ	nà xiē	zhè	zhè xiē	zhè lǐ

• • • • • • • • • • • • • • • • • • • • • • • • • • • • • •

Exercise 2

Identify the Chinese which correctly translates each of
these English sentences. Write it in the space provided
and say the Chinese out loud.

1) This is my dad. （那是我的爸爸，
这是我的爸爸，那是我的妈妈）

• •

2) Who is that? （这是谁，那是谁，
她是谁）

• •

3) I'm here. （我在那里，他在这里，
我在这里）

• •

4) He's sitting over there. （他坐在那里，
他在那里，她坐在那里）

• •

Lesson 9

5) These people left yesterday.

（这些人今天走了，这些人昨天走了，
那些人昨天走了）

. . . .

6) Those people have already arrived. （这些人已经
来了, 那些人已经来了, 哪些人已经来了）

. . . .

7) This person is reading a book. （这个人在写书，
那个人在看书，这个人在看书）

. . . .

Exercise 3

Translate these sentences into English. Say the Chinese
out loud first.

1) 这是我的父母。 . . . .

2) 那是他们的。 . . . .

3) 这些是我们的。 . . . .

4) 你的在这里。 . . . .

5) 他们的在那里。 . . . .

Lesson 10 ~ *Some measure words*

*N*ow we are going to learn how to write some measure words. There is one which you have learned already:

个	gè	a general purpose measure word

Some commonly used measure words are:

只	zhī	measure word for birds and animals
支	zhī	measure word for pens, pencils, cigarettes and long cylindrical things
本	běn	measure word for books and magazines
张	zhāng	measure word for flat things like paper
杯	bēi	cup; glass
块	kuài	piece; block

 *character building*

只	丨	冂	口	尸	只

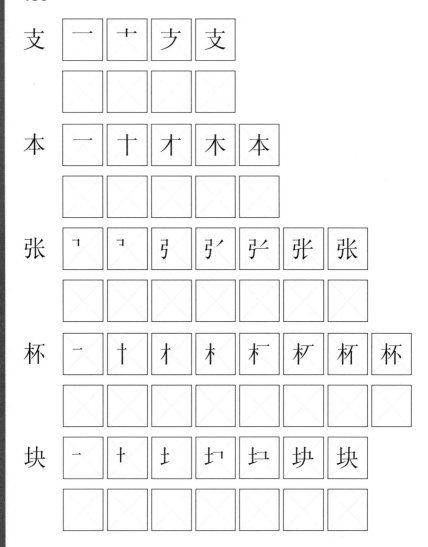

Exercise 1

Now look at the following pictures. Fill in the blanks with the correct measure words. Say the Chinese out loud as you do this.

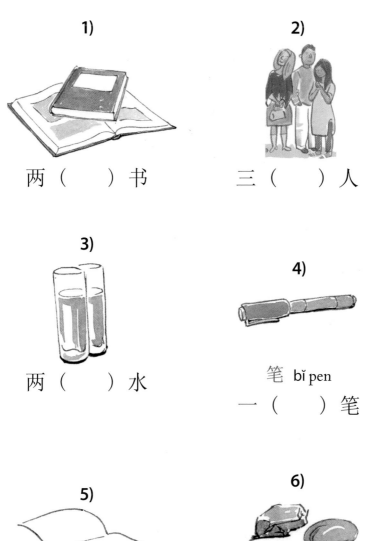

1)

两（　　）书

2)

三（　　）人

3)

两（　　）水

4)

笔　bǐ pen

一（　　）笔

5)

纸　zhǐ piece of paper

一（　　）纸

6)

石头　shí tou stone

三（　　）石头

7)

鸟 niǎo bird

五（　　）鸟

Exercise 2

The measure words for these pictures have got jumbled up. Can you sort them out?

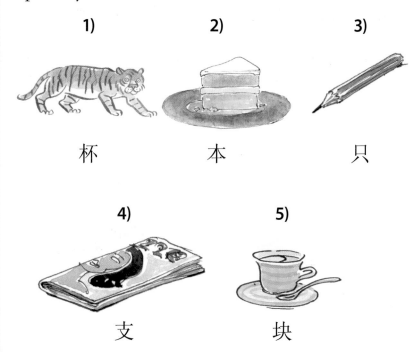

1)   **2)**   **3)**

杯   本   只

4)   **5)**

支   块

Lesson 10

Exercise 3

Translate these sentences into English. Say the Chinese out loud as well.

1) 我有三本书。

· ·

2) 我的姐姐有两个儿子。

· ·

3) 那里有一杯水。

· ·

4) 这里有三支笔。

· ·

5) 他在一张纸上写字。

· ·

Lesson 10

Lesson 11 ~ *More question words*

In this lesson we are going to continue learning some more question words.

多少？	duō shǎo?	how many?; how much?
怎么 (样)？	zěn me (yàng)?	how?
哪里？	ná lǐ?	where?
谁的？	shéi de?	whose?

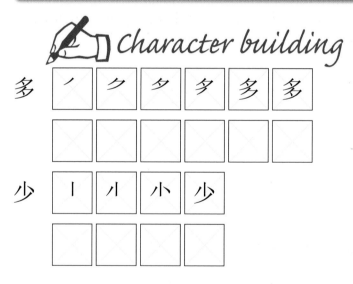

Character building

多	ノ	ク	夕	夕	多	多

少	丨	小	小	少

Here are a few useful everyday phrases to memorize:

怎么回事?	Zěn me huí shì?	What's the matter?
你怎么了?	Nǐ zěn me le?	What's the matter with you?
你多大了?	Nǐ duō dà le?	How old are you?
生日快乐!	Shēngrì kuàilè!	Happy birthday!

Now let's do some exercises.

Exercise 1

Hanzi and English have got jumbled up. Can you write the correct English in the space provided?

1)	**2)**	**3)**	**4)**
哪里?	怎么?	谁的?	多少?
whose?	how many?	how?	where?

. . . .

Exercise 2

Choose the correct Chinese translation from the three possibilities. Say the Chinese out loud.

1) How many books have you got?

（他有多少本书?, 你有多少本书?,

她有多少本书?）

. . . .

Lesson 11

2) Where did he go yesterday?

（她昨天去哪里了?，

他昨天去哪里了?，他去哪里了?）

. . . .

3) Whose pen is it? （那是谁的笔?，

这是谁的笔?，那是一支笔吗?）

. . . .

4) How many children do you have? （你有多少个孩

子?，你有孩子谁的?， 你有多少人?）

. . . .

5) What's happened to him? （她怎么了?，

他怎么了?，他去哪里了?）

. . . .

6) How old is she? （他多大了？，她多老了?，

她多大了?）

. . . .

Exercise 3

Look at these pictures and answer the questions by filling in the missing character(s).

1) What are you doing?

你在做……？

……在……。

2) How old are you?

你……了？

生日 快乐

我……岁。

You'll see that Chinese often uses Arabic numbers too. And you need to use the character 岁 suì, which means 'year' when saying what your age is.

3) Where did you go yesterday?

你. . . . . 去. . . . . 了？

我. . . . . . 。

4) Mum has lost her book.

爸爸，这是. . . . . .书？

那是. . . . . .的。

Lesson 12 ~ *Some adjectives*

In this lesson we are going to learn some common adjectives.

好	hǎo	good; fine; nice
坏	huài	bad
多	duō	lots (of); many; much
少	shǎo	few; fewer; less
美	měi	beautiful, pretty, lovely
丑	chǒu	ugly

In Chinese it's common to put a modifier, a word like hěn (very), in front of the adjective. For example, 'She is beautiful' is normally translated as 她很美.

New words

消 息	xiāo xī	news
很	hěn	very

Exercise 1

English and hanzi are jumbled up. Can you put the English under the right hanzi?

Lesson 12

1)	**2)**	**3)**	**4)**	**5)**	**6)**
少	多	美	坏	好	丑
good	ugly	few	much	bad	beautiful

. . . . .　　. . . .　　. . . .　　. . . .　　. . . .　　. . . .

Exercise 2

Write down the opposites of these characters. Say the words out loud.

1) 少 . . . .

2) 丑 . . . .

3) 好 . . . .

4) 哭 . . . .

5) 去 . . . .

Exercise 3

Underline the correct translation from the three possibilities.

1) My younger sister said I am her good sister.

（我的妹妹说我是她姐姐，

我的妹妹说我是他的好姐姐，

我的妹妹说我是她的好姐姐）

2) I have some bad news. （我有一个消息，
我有一个坏消息，我有一个好消息）

3) He has lots of children. （他没有孩子，
他有很少孩子，他有很多孩子）

4) There are fewer people on that side.
（这边的人少，那边的人少，那边的人多）

5) This man is very ugly. （这个人很丑，
这个人真美，这个人不丑）

Lesson 13 ~ *Some more adjectives*

*I*n this lesson we are going to learn some more common
adjectives.

对	duì	right, correct
错	cuò	wrong
长	cháng	long
短	duǎn	short
冷	lěng	cold
热	rè	hot

In Chinese we sometimes put the particle 了 at the end of a sentence to indicate a fact or simply to express a past tense. For example, 我错了 means 'I am wrong' and 他走了 means 'He left'.

Now let's do some exercises.

Exercise 1

English and hanzi are jumbled up. Can you put the correct English under each hanzi?

1) 短	2) 错	3) 热	4) 长	5) 对	6) 冷
hot	long	correct	cold	short	wrong

. . . . .　　. . . . .　　. . . . .　　. . . . .　　. . . . .　　. . . . .

Exercise 2

Write the opposites of the following characters. Say the Chinese out loud as you do this.

1) 这 . . . . . .

2) 长 . . . . . .

3) 冷 . . . . . .

4) 对 . . . . . .

Lesson 13

5) 多　.....

6) 美　.....

7) 坏　.....

Exercise 3

Underline the correct translation from the three possibilities.

1) She did right. （他做对了，她对了，
   她做对了）

2) He said he was wrong. （他说她错了，
   他说我错了，他说他错了）

3) It is very cold today. （今天很冷，今天不冷，
   今天很热）

4) a glass of hot water （一杯冷水，
   一杯热水，一杯水）

5) I have long hair. （我有长头发，
   我有短头发，我头发长）

Lesson 14 ~ *Some common modifiers*

*I*n this lesson we are going to learn some more modifiers, like 很 in Lesson 12. In Chinese these are normally combined with adjectives.

比 较	bǐ jiào	relatively ; fairly
非 常	fēi cháng	extremely
太	tài	too; very
特 别	tè bié	particularly; specially

Now let's do some exercises.

Exercise 1

Use the hanzi (汉字) you have learned above to put the correct English under each hanzi.

1)	2)	3)	4)	5)
非常	很	比较	特别	太
too	particularly	extremely	very	fairly

. . . .

Exercise 2

Underline the correct translation from the three possibilities given.

1) It's too hot today. （今天很热， 今天很冷， 今天太热了）

2) This one is fairly long. （这个很长， 这个比较长， 这个长）

3) Here comes some very bad news. （有个坏消息， 有个消息， 有个很坏的消息）

4) She is very beautiful. （她非常丑， 她非常美， 他非常美）

5) Last December was extremely cold. （去年十一月很冷， 去年十二月很冷， 去年十二月特别冷）

There are several characters pronounced hen (but with different tones). Circle the one that means 'very'.

Puzzle

1) 恨

2) 狠

4) 痕

3) 很

Lesson 15 ~ *More function words*

*I*n this lesson we are going to learn the characters for some more key function words.

又	yòu	again
也	yě	also; too; as well
都	dōu	both; all
不	bù	no; not
没	méi	not; have not
对	duì	to; at

méi, not bù, is used for 'not' when talking about the past or in combination with 有 yǒu

In Block 2 Lesson 13 we learned the character 对 meaning 'correct, right'. In this lesson the same character occurs again, here meaning 'to' or 'at', for example, 她对我说 'she said *to* me'.

Now let's do some exercises.

Exercise 1

English and 汉字 have got jumbled up. Can you put the correct English under each 汉字?

1)	2)	3)	4)	5)	6)
都	对	也	没	不	又
not	also	both	no	to	again

· · · · ·   · · · ·   · · · ·   · · · ·   · · · ·   · · · ·

Exercise 2

Circle the correct translation from the three possibilities.
Say your answer out loud where no pinyin is given.

1) She is smiling at me.

（她在笑， 她笑了， 她在对我笑）

2) Mā ma yòu huí lái le.

（妈妈回来了， 妈妈回去了， 妈妈又回来了）

3) This one is also very good.

（这个很好， 这个也好， 这个也很好）

4) Jīn tiān bù lěng.

（今天不冷, 今天不热， 昨天不热）

5) I didn't ask her.

（我不问她， 我没问她， 我没问他）

6) Grandpa and grandma are both not coming.

（爷爷和奶奶都来了, 爷爷和奶奶都不来了, 爷爷和妈妈都不来了）

Lesson 15

There are several characters pronounced mei (but with different tones). Circle the one that means 'not'.

Puzzle

1) 每

7) 煤

2) 美

6) 妹

3) 梅

5) 没

4) 枚

Lesson 16 ~ *Negatives and questions*

*I*n this lesson, we are going to learn a pair of useful negative expressions composed of the characters 不 and 没.

不 是	bú shì	no; not; am not/is not/are not etc
没 有	méi yǒu	not; have not; has not

We'll also learn a common hanzi 吗 *used to turn sentences into questions.*

吗	ma	question word

Lesson 16

Exercise 1

Look at the following pictures and then fill in the missing characters in the sentences.

1)

那……你妈妈吗?

不是, 她……我妈妈。

2)

这个……我的杯子……?

这……你的杯子, 那个……你的。

3)

你.... 多少个孩子?

我......孩子。

Exercise 2

Translate the following sentences into Chinese characters and write down the answers. Say the Chinese out loud.

1) She is not my younger sister. She is my older sister.

. . . .

2) My grandpa is not reading. He is writing.

Use 没 or 没有

. . . .

3) Did he come back yesterday?

. . . .

Lesson 16

4) I don't have that book.

. . . .

When using words for 'my' or 'his' etc with family members you can leave out the 的.

Lesson 17 ~ *Some important verbs*

*I*n this lesson we're going to learn some important characters for words like 'want' and 'can'. We will also rehearse some of the things we have learned so far.

想	xiǎng	to think; to want
要	yào	to want; to need
会	huì	will; to be able to
能	néng	can, to be able to
得	děi	must, to have to
请	qǐng	to ask; to invite; please

The character 想 combined with 要 means 'would like'. For example, I would like a glass of water 我想要一杯水.

Let's do some exercises.

Exercise 1

Look at the English translation first and then fill in the empty bracket with the correct character(s). For example:

He said,"I think you are right."

他说，"我（　）你是对的。"
他说，"我　想　你是对的。"

1) He wants that long one.

   他（　　）那个长的。

2) I must go home tomorrow.

   我明天（　　）回家了。

3) My younger brother is able to write.

   我的弟弟（　　）写字了。

4) I'll come. 我（　　）来的。

5) She asked, "When do you want to go back?"

   她问，"你（　　）什么时候回去?"

6) Please sit down. （　　）坐。

7) Grandpa can't come tomorrow.

爷爷明天（　　）来了。

8) Grandma won't be coming the day after tomorrow.

奶奶后天（　　）来了。

Exercise 2

Translate the following sentences into Chinese. Say your answers out loud as you write them down.

1) He wants to read, he doesn't want to talk.

. . . .

2) My older sister wants to meet me tomorrow.

. . . .

3) He won't come tomorrow.

. . . .

4) You can't go home tomorrow.

. . . .

5) I invited her to come here.

. . . .

Lesson 18 ~ *Some more verbs*

*I*n this lesson we're going to learn some more important characters for commonly used Chinese verbs.

知 道	zhī dào	to know
可 以	kě yǐ	may; can
必 须	bì xū	must; to have to
需 要	xū yào	to need; to require; to demand
应 该	yīng gāi	should; must; ought to

Exercise 1

Look at the English translation first and then fill in the empty bracket with the correct character(s). For example:

He said to me, "I know I am wrong."

他对我说，　"我（　）我错了。"

他对我说，　"我知道我错了。"

1) I don't know when he's arriving tomorrow morning.

我（　　　）他明天上午什么时候来。

2) I can meet you at 4pm.

我（　　）在下午四点见你。

3) You can't do that. 你（　　）那样做。

4) I must go! 我（　　）走了!

5) I need a piece of paper. 我（　　）一张纸。

6) You shouldn't have gone yesterday. 你昨天

（　　）走。

Exercise 2

Write the following sentences in Chinese characters. And say them out loud, where no pinyin is given.

1) I don't know who you are.

. . . .

2) You can't come here tomorrow.

. . . .

3) You must go home at 2pm.

. . . .

4) Tā yīng gāi zài zhè lǐ jiàn wǒ.

. . . .

5) I don't know how many books she needs.

. . . .

Lesson 18

Lesson 19 ~ *Greetings*

*L*et's look at some very commonly used Chinese greetings.

你 好	nǐ hǎo	hello
早 上 好	zǎo shàng hǎo	good morning
下 午 好	xià wǔ hǎo	good afternoon
晚 上 好	wǎn shàng hǎo	good evening
晚 安	wǎn ān	good night
再 见	zài jiàn	goodbye
回 头 见	huí tóu jiàn	see you later
明 天 见	míng tiān jiàn	see you tomorrow

Sometimes people use 回见 instead of 回头见 to say 'see you later'.

Exercise 1

English and 汉字 have got jumbled up again. Can you write the correct English under each 汉字?

1)	2)	3)	4)	5)	6)
早上好	你好	晚安	再见	晚上好	回头见
good evening	bye-bye	see you later	hello	good morning	good night

· · · · ·   · · · · ·   · · · · ·   · · · · ·   · · · · ·   · · · · ·

Exercise 2

Underline the correct translation from the three possibilities.

1) We should say 'good morning' when it is morning.

（我们应该在早上说‘晚上好’，

我们应该在早上说‘早上好’，

我们应该说‘早上好’）

2) We should say 'good afternoon' when it is afternoon.

（我们应该在下午说‘早上好’，

我们应该在下午说‘下午好’，

我们应该在晚上说‘下午好’）

3) We should say 'good evening' when it is evening.

（我们应该在晚上说‘早上好’，

我们应该在晚上说‘晚上好’，

我们应该在下午说‘晚上好’）

Lesson 19

4) She said to me, "See you later".

（她对我说"明天见"，她说"回头见"，
她对我说"回头见"）

5) His mother said to him, "Good night."

（他妈妈对她说"晚安"，
他妈妈对他说"晚安"，
他妈妈对他说"晚上好"）

Exercise 3

In these pictures the pinyin and the characters have got jumbled up. Can you sort them out?

1) wǎn ān 你好

2) nǐ hǎo 再见

3) zài jiàn 早上好

4) zǎo shàng hǎo 晚安

Lesson 20 ~ *Some common expressions*

*I*n this lesson we are going to learn some important expressions which you will encounter in everyday life.

对不起	duì bù qǐ	sorry; pardon me
没关系	méi guān xi	it's all right; it doesn't matter; never mind
谢谢（你）	xiè xiè (nǐ)	thank you
非常感谢	fēi cháng gǎn xiè	thanks a lot; thank you very much
不客气	bú kè qi	you're welcome; don't mention it
没问题	méi wèn tí	no problem
劳驾	láo jià	excuse me *(to attract attention)*
多保重	duō bǎo zhòng	take care
好的	hǎo de	ok

Now let's do some exercises.

Exercise 1

Pinyin and hanzi have got jumbled up. Can you write the correct pinyin under each hanzi?

1)	2)	3)	4)	5)
没关系	对不起	劳驾	谢谢	多保重

láo jià   xiè xiè   duō bǎo zhòng   duì bù qǐ   méi guān xi

. . . .

Exercise 2

Look at the English translation first and then fill in the empty bracket with the correct character(s). Say your answers out loud when you write them down. For example:

I should say sorry to my younger sister.
我应该对我妹妹说（   ）。
我应该对我妹妹说对不起。
Wǒ yīng gāi duì wǒ mèi mei shuō duì bù qǐ.

1) A: I'm sorry.

   A: （   ）

   B: It's all right.

   B: （   ）

2) She said, "You are so nice, thanks a lot!"

她说，"你太好了!(   )!"

I said, "You are welcome."

我说，"(   )"。

3) A: I would like a glass of water.

    B: No problem.

    A: 我想要一杯水。

    B: (   )。

4) Excuse me, this is mine, and that one is yours.

(   )，这个是我的，那个是你的。

5) Excuse me, what time is it?

(   )，几点了?

6) A: See you tomorrow.

    A: 明天见。

    B: Ok. Take care.

    B: 好的。(   )。

Lesson 20

Block 3

Quiz

1. Which is the character for 'he'? Is it
   a) 你 **b)** 他 **c)** 她?

2. Both of these are pronounced zuò.
   Which one means 'to do' or 'to make'?
   a) 坐 **b)** 做

3. How is 回 pronounced? Is it
   a) qù **b)** huà **c)** huí?

4. Complete this hanzi wèn meaning 'to ask'.

5. Which of these means 'to go home'? Is it
   a) 回去 **b)** 回家 **c)** 回来?

6. This is March and you were born in January.
   Is your next birthday
   a) 今年三月 **b)** 去年一月 **c)** 明年一月?

7. Which of the following means 'why?' Is it
   a) 为什么? **b)** 谁? **c)** 什么?

8. What is wrong with this sentence about your brothers?   她们是我的哥哥

9. What is the measure word for books? Is it
   a) 杯 bēi **b)** 本 běn **c)** 支 zhī?

10. Which of these is the opposite of 美 měi. Is it
    a) 好 hǎo **b)** 冷 lěng **c)** 丑 chǒu?

Lesson 1 ~ *Clothes*

N̄ow we're going to learn some characters for clothes.

衣 服　yī fu　clothes

上 衣　shàng yī

大 衣　dà yī

裤 子　kù zi

鞋 子　xié zi

袜 子　wà zi

手 套　shǒu tào

New hanzi

Here are two new measure words you need to know.

件	jiàn	a measure word for sweaters, tops, coats etc	两件上衣	two jackets
双	shuāng	pair	一双袜子	a pair of socks

Now let's do some exercises.

Exercise 1

The following captions have got jumbled up. Can you rearrange them with the correct characters?

1)   2)   3)

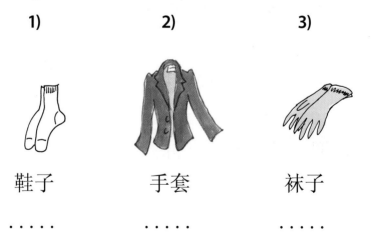

鞋子   手套   袜子

· · · · ·   · · · · ·   · · · · ·

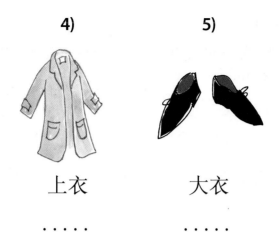

4) 上衣

· · · · ·

5) 大衣

· · · · ·

Exercise 2

Select the correct measure word from the three possibilities. And say the Chinese out loud.

1) 三　（双, 件, 条）鞋子

2) 一　（个, 件, 块）大衣

3) 两　（只, 张, 双）手套

4) 六　（个, 支, 只）人

5) 四　（条, 块, 双）裤子

Exercise 3

Translate the following sentences into English. Say the Chinese out loud when you do this.

1) 我有两双手套。

. . . .

2) 这是我姐姐的大衣，不是我的。

. . . .

3) 这是谁的鞋子？

. . . .

4) 这条裤子很长。

. . . .

5) 我的袜子在哪里？

. . . .

Lesson 2 ~ *Colours*

*I*n this lesson we are going to learn some colour words.

白 bái   红 hóng   粉 fěn

绿 lǜ   黄 huáng   蓝 lán

紫 zǐ   黑 hēi

When using these colour words we normally combine another word 色 to express the specific colour. For example, "green clothes" is 绿色的衣服.

New hanzi

色	sè	colour

Exercise 1

Match each colour word with its correct translation.

1)	**2)**	**3)**	**4)**
紫色	黄色	粉色	白色
red	black	green	blue

. . . .

5)	**6)**	**7)**	**8)**
红色	绿色	黑色	蓝色
yellow	pink	purple	white

. . . .

Lesson 2

Exercise 2

Describe the following pictures by writing down the
correct colour word in the space provided. Don't forget to
add the colour word 色.   And say your answers out loud.

Example:

蓝色 lán sè

1) . . . .   2) . . . .   3) . . . .

4) . . . .   5) . . . .   6) . . . .

7) . . . .   8) . . . .

Lesson 2

Exercise 3

Read the English sentence first and complete the following Chinese sentence by filling in the missing characters. Read the Chinese sentences out loud.

Example: He has a black coat.

他有一件（　　　）的大衣。　　　黑色
Tā yǒu yí jiàn hēi sè de dà yī.

1) I have a pair of blue gloves and my younger sister has

yellow ones. 我有一双（　　　）的手套，我

妹妹有一双（　　　）的。

2) My jacket is white. 我的上衣是（　　　）的。

3) I didn't see her red shoes.

我（　　　）看见她那双（　　　）的鞋子。

4) I want that pink one. 我想要那件（　　　）的。

的 can be used to avoid repeating a noun, like using 'ones' in 'yellow ones.'

Lesson 3 ~ *Plants and fruit*

In this lesson we are going to learn some characters for plants and fruit.

花 huā flower 　　草 cǎo grass 　　树 shù tree

水果 shuǐ guǒ
fruit

梨 lí pear

桔子 jú zi
orange

苹果 píng guǒ
apple

桃子 táo zi
peach

香蕉 xiāng jiāo
banana

New hanzi

喜欢 一些	xǐ huān yì xiē	like some	我喜欢桔子 一些花	I like oranges some flowers

Exercise 1

Match each character with its English translation.

1) 桃子 tree	**2)** 苹果 fruit	**3)** 草 pear	**4)** 树 banana

. . . .

5) 水果 flower	**6)** 梨 grass	**7)** 花 peach	**8)** 香蕉 apple

. . . .

Exercise 2

Translate the following into English, reading the Chinese out loud.

1) 三个梨

. . . .

2) 红色的苹果

. . . .

3) 很多紫色的花

. . . .

4) 一些桔子

. . . .

5) 你喜欢什么水果?

. . . .

6) 我喜欢香蕉。

. . . .

7) 我的爸爸不喜欢桃子。

. . . .

8) 那里有一些花。

. . . .

Lesson 3

There are several characters pronounced hua (but with different tones). Identify the one that means 'flower' from this list.

Puzzle

1) 华

2) 桦

5) 骅

3) 花

4) 化

Lesson 4 ~ *Seasons and the weather*

In this lesson we are going to learn some characters for the seasons and the weather.

春 chūn spring

夏 xià summer

秋 qiū autumn

冬 dōng winter

雨 yǔ rain

雪 xuě snow

The four seasons are normally written like this in Chinese characters:

春 天	chūn tiān	spring
夏 天	xià tiān	summer
秋 天	qiū tiān	autumn
冬 天	dōng tiān	winter

And we use 下雨 and 下雪 for "raining" or "snowing".

下 雨	raining	下 雨 了	It's raining.
下 雪	snowing	下 雪 了	It's snowing.

The character 下, which you first met in Block 1 Lesson 6 can also mean 'fall'.

Exercise 1

Put these Chinese captions against the correct pictures.

1) 冬天 . . . .   **2)** 夏天 . . . .

3) 春天 . . . .   **4)** 下雨 . . . .

Exercise 2

Write down in the blank space the correct season that the following months belong to.

1) 七月 . . . .   **4)** 四月 . . . .

2) 十月 . . . .   **5)** 八月 . . . .

3) 十二月 . . . .

Lesson 4

Exercise 3

Select the character(s) in the brackets which will make a complete sentence when put in the space.

1) 春天 . . . . . . 了。(下, 回, 来)

2) . . . . . . 雨了。(打, 上, 下)

3) . . . . . . 天冷, ... 天热。(冬, 秋; 春, 冬; 冬, 夏)

4) 我 . . . . . . 秋天。(喜欢, 走, 去)

5) 我会 . . . . . . 今年冬天回来。(和, 在, 从)

Lesson 5 ~ *In the kitchen*

*N*ow we are going to learn some characters for things you'll find in the kitchen.

盘子 pán zi
plate

碟子 dié zi
saucer

碗 wǎn
bowl

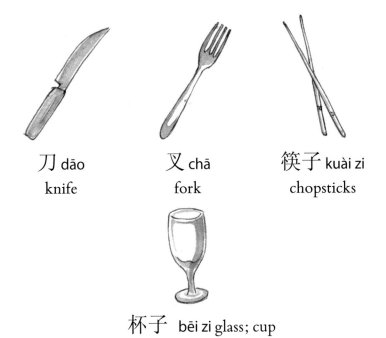

刀 dāo
knife

叉 chā
fork

筷子 kuài zi
chopsticks

杯子 bēi zi glass; cup

Remember the following measure word.

| 把 | bǎ | 两 把 刀 | two knives |

Exercise 1

Write the correct Chinese caption against each picture, saying the captions out loud.

1) 刀 . . . . . .   2) 碗 . . . .

3) 叉 . . . .

4) 杯子 . . . .

5) 筷子 . . . .

6) 盘子 . . . .

7) 碟子 . . . .

Exercise 2

Write out the correct measure word from the three possibilities.

1) 两...盘子 （个, 本, 张） . . . .

2) 一...碟子 （双, 块, 个） . . . .

3) 三...刀 （把, 支, 双） . . . .

4) 两...筷子　（张，双，本）．．．．．．．．．．．

5) 一...叉子　（块，条，把）．．．．．．．．．．．

Exercise 3

Rearrange these Chinese phrases so as to correctly describe the pictures.

1) 两个蓝色的盘子

．．．．．．．．．．．．．．．．．．．

2) 一个红色的碟子

．．．．．．．．．．．．．．．．．．．

3) 两个黄色的碗

．．．．．．．．．．．．．．．．．．．

4) 一双绿色的筷子

．．．．．．．．．．．．．．．．．．．

Lesson 5

Lesson 6 ~ *Furniture*

*I*n this lesson we're going to learn some characters for furniture.

桌子 zhuō zi

椅子 yǐ zi

床 chuáng

门 mén

窗户 chuāng hu window

地毯 dì tǎn carpet

地板 dì bǎn floor

衣柜 yī guì wardrobe

You'll need to remember these measure words.

张	zhāng	*as in:* 一张桌子；一张床
扇	shàn	*as in:* 一扇窗户
把	bǎ	*as in:* 一把椅子
块	kuài	*as in:* 一块地毯

Exercise 1

Write the correct Chinese caption against each picture, saying the captions out loud.

1) 黑色的门

. . . .

2) 黄色的椅子

. . . .

3) 红色的地毯

. . . .

4) 黄色的桌子

. . . .

5) 绿色的窗户

. . . .

Lesson 6

Exercise 2

Translate into English

1) 在桌子上 . . . .

2) 坐在椅子上。 . . . .

3) 在衣柜里 . . . .

4) 在地板上 . . . .

There are several characters pronounced men (but with different tones). Which one means 'door'?

Puzzle

1) 们

5) 门 2) 钔

4) 闷 3) 扪

Lesson 7 ~ *Birds*

*I*n this lesson we're going to learn some characters for birds.

鸟 niǎo bird

鸡 jī

鸭 yā

鹅 é

天鹅 tiān é

乌鸦 wū yā crow

Exercise 1

Rearrange the following jumbled-up captions.

1) 天鹅 . . . . . .   **2)** 鸡 . . . . . .   **3)** 鸭 . . . . . .

4) 鹅 . . . . . .   **5)** 鸟 . . . . . .

Lesson 7

Exercise 2

Write down the common part of the following
characters.

鸡   鸭   鹅   鸦

> You can't *hear* that this is a common element. But
> you can *see* it.

Exercise 3

Translate these into English.

1) 树上有两只鸟。

. . . .

2) 他昨天看见一只乌鸦。

. . . .

3) 我喜欢白天鹅。

. . . .

4) 那里有三只鸡。

. . . .

Lesson 8 ~ *Animals*

*I*n this lesson we're going to learn some characters for animals.

猫 māo

狗 gǒu

狼 láng

猴 hóu

猪 zhū

虎 hǔ

牛 niú

马 mǎ

羊 yáng

Lesson 8

Notice that the first five characters have one common part, 犭 which in Chinese normally indicates a connection with animals.

Normally we use the measure word 只 for animals. For example 一只猫 or 一只狼. But there are a few exceptions. Remember the following measure words:

| 头 | tóu | 一头牛；一头猪 |
| 匹 | pǐ | 一匹马 |

Now let's do some exercises.

Exercise 1

Rearrange the following jumbled captions.

1) 狼 . . . . . .　　2) 猴 . . . . . .　　3) 狗 . . . . . .

4) 猪 . . . . . .　　5) 猫 . . . . . .　　6) 虎 . . . . . .

Exercise 2

Look at the following pictures and fill in the empty brackets with the correct measure words and animal words.

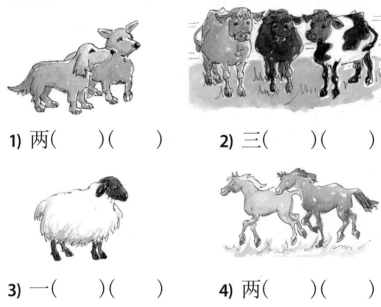

1) 两（　　）（　　　）　　2) 三（　　）（　　　）

3) 一（　　）（　　　）　　4) 两（　　）（　　　）

Exercise 3

Read these sentences out in Chinese and then translate them into English.

1) 这是谁的猫？　这是我的。

．．．．．．．．．．．．．．．．．．．．．．．．．．．．．．．．

2) 我有一只黑色的狗。

．．．．．．．．．．．．．．．．．．．．．．．．．．．．．．．．

3) 那不是我的马。

. . . .

4) 他有几只羊？　他有二十四只羊。

. . . .

Lesson 9 ~ *Transport*

In this lesson we will learn some characters for means of getting around.

飞机　fēi jī

汽车　qì chē

卡车　kǎ chē

公共汽车　gōng gòng qì chē

火车 huǒ chē

出租车 chū zū chē

船 chuán

自行车 zì xíng chē

Remember the following phrases.

工作	gōng zuò	to work; job 他在工作。 He's working.
在…上	zài … shàng	in, at, on 他在火车上工作。 He's working on the trains.

Exercise 1

Rearrange the following jumbled captions.

1) 汽车

2) 飞机

3) 卡车

. . . .

Lesson 9

4) 公共汽车　　5) 自行车　　6) 船

. . . .　　. . . . .　　. . . . .

Exercise 2

Identify the correct translation from the three possibilities given and then write it down, saying the Chinese out loud.

1) His older brother works on the buses.

他的哥哥在公共汽车上看书。

他的弟弟在火车上工作。

他的哥哥在公共汽车上工作。

. . . .

2) I don't have a bike.

我不需要自行车。

我没有自行车。

我想要自行车。

. . . .

Lesson 9

3) I want a job working on a boat.

我想在船上工作。

我不想在船上工作。

我不要在船上工作。

. . . .

Exercise 3

Look at the pictures below, answer the Chinese questions and write the correct Chinese characters down. Here are some new hanzi that you will need for this.

哪一个?	nǎ yí gè? which?	快	kuài fast
大	dà big	慢	màn slow
小	xiǎo small	不同	bù tóng different

1) 哪一个大?　　　2) 哪一个小?

3) 哪一个快？

4) 哪一个慢？

5) 哪一个不同？

Lesson 10 ~ *Some everyday objects*

*I*n this lesson we're going to learn some characters for everyday objects.

冰箱 **bīng xiāng**

洗衣机 **xǐ yī jī**

手表 shǒu biǎo

电脑 diàn nǎo

电视 diàn shì

电话 diàn huà

手机 shǒu jī

电灯 diàn dēng

The character 电 means electric.

Remember these measure words.

台	tái measure word for bigger machines	一台电脑 one computer
块	kuài piece	一块手表 one watch

Lesson 10

Exercise 1

Rearrange the following jumbled captions.

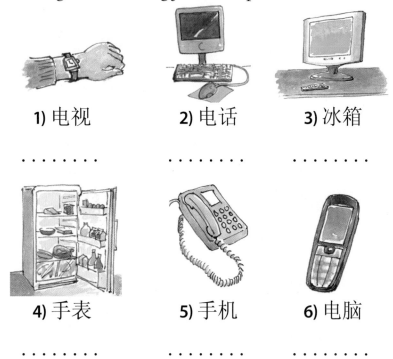

1) 电视

2) 电话

3) 冰箱

. . . .

. . . .

. . . .

4) 手表

5) 手机

6) 电脑

. . . .

. . . .

. . . .

Exercise 2

Identify the correct translation from the three possibilities given and then write it down, saying the Chinese out loud.

1) The apple's on the fridge.

水果在冰箱里。
苹果在冰箱上。
苹果在冰箱里。

. . . .

2) My computer is black.

我的电脑是黑色的。

我的冰箱是黑色的。

我的电话是黑色的。

· ·

3) Your watch is on the desk.

你的手表在椅子上。

你的手表在桌子上。

你的手表在桌子下。

· ·

4) I'm watching TV.

他看电视了。

我在看书。

我在看电视。

· ·

Exercise 3

Fill in the missing characters in the empty brackets so as to give correct translations.

1) What's that? That's a fridge.

那是 （　　　）？　那是（　　　）。

2) Is this your watch? No, that's not my watch. Mine is red.

这是你的（　　　　）吗?　（　　　　），

这（　　　　）我的（　　　　）。

我的是（　　　　）的。

3) Whose computer is this? My younger brother's.

这是（　　　　）的电脑？　我（　　　　）。

4) I don't have a telephone at home.

我家里没有（　　　　）。

Lesson 11 ~ *Writing materials*

*I*n *this lesson we're going to learn some characters for writing materials.*

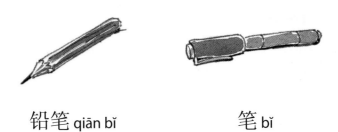

铅笔 qiān bǐ　　　　　　　笔 bǐ

尺子 chǐ zi

橡皮 xiàng pí

纸 zhǐ

笔记本 bǐ jì běn

课本 kè běn
textbook

Remember these measure words.

一支铅笔	一张纸
一把尺子	一个笔记本
一块橡皮	

Lesson 11

Exercise 1

Rearrange the following jumbled captions.

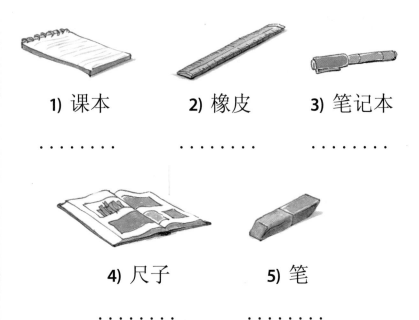

1) 课本

2) 橡皮

3) 笔记本

. . . .

. . . .

. . . .

4) 尺子

5) 笔

. . . .

. . . .

Exercise 2

Identify the correct translation from the following three possibilities and write your answer down.

1) two rubbers

两份橡皮， 两块橡皮， 两条橡皮

. . . .

2) one pen

一只笔， 一支笔， 一支笔

. . . .

3) three notebooks

三张笔记本，　三只笔记本，　三个笔记本

. . . .

4) one ruler

一把尺子，　一件尺子，　一张尺子

. . . .

Exercise 3

Complete the following translations by filling in the missing characters.

1) I don't need a pen.

我不需要（　　　　　）。

2) I need a pencil.

我需要（　　　　　）。

3) Her textbook is on the desk.

（　　　　）的（　　　　　）在桌子上。

4) Excuse me, who knows where my notebook is?

（　　　　），　谁知道我的（　　　　）

在（　　　　）？

5) Do you know where the paper is?

你知道（　　　　）在（　　　　　）吗?

Lesson 11

Lesson 12 ~ *Professions*

*I*n this lesson we'll learn some characters for professions or occupations.

老 师 lǎo shī teacher

学 生 xué shēng student

医 生 yī shēng doctor

护 士 hù shi nurse

法 官 fǎ guān judge

律 师 lǜ shī lawyer

New hanzi

位	wèi	measure word for people with a specific profession (although 个 can also be used) 一位医生 one doctor

Exercise 1

Rearrange the following jumbled captions.

1) 护士

2) 律师

3) 法官

. . . .

4) 老师

5) 学生

. . . .

Exercise 2

Underline the correct translation from the following three possibilities.

1) one teacher

一个律师， 一位老师， 一只老师

2) three coats

三个大衣， 三件大衣， 三件衣服

3) one notebook

一个笔记本， 一只笔记本， 一张笔记本

4) two jackets

两条上衣， 两件上衣， 两个上衣

5) one pair of shoes

一只鞋子， 一个鞋子， 一双鞋子

Exercise 3

Complete the following translation by filling in the missing words.

1) On the left is a teacher, on the right a doctor.

左边是一位（　　　　　）， 右边是一位

（　　　　　）。

2) The nurse has left. （   ）走了。

3) There are two judges over there.

那里有两位（   ）。

4) The lawyer asked her, 'When did you go home

yesterday evening?' （   ）问她，

'昨天（   ）你（）回家的？'

5) The three students are reading.

（   ）在看书。

Lesson 13 ~ *Jobs*

*I*n this lesson we're going to learn some more hanzi
for jobs.

警 察 jǐng chá policeman   农 民 nóng mín farmer

公 务 员 gōng wù yuán
civil servant

工 人 gōng rén
factory worker

军 人 jūn rén
soldier

商 人 shāng rén
businessman

character building

The hanzi for jǐng chá are quite complex. Here are the strokes.

警 一 十 艹 产 芍 芍 苟 苟

苟ノ 苟ㄏ 苟ㄅ 敬 敬 敬 警 警

警 警 警

察 丶 八 宀 宀 宀 宀 宀 宀

突 突 突 窣 察 察

Exercise 1

Can you sort out these jumbled captions.

1) 商人   **2)** 公务员   **3)** 工人

· · · · · · · ·   · · · · · · · ·   · · · · · · · ·

4) 农民   **5)** 军人

· · · · · · · ·   · · · · · · · ·

Exercise 2

Underline the correct answer from the following three possibilities.

1) My dad is a policeman.

我爸爸是一位 · · · · · · · · · · · · · · · · · ·

（工人，警察，农民）。

Lesson 13

2) His older brother is a businessman.

他哥哥是一位 . . . .
（商人，军人，公务员）。

3) She is a civil servant.

她是一位 . . . .
（警察，公务员，工人）。

4) My mum is a factory worker.

我妈妈是一位 . . . .
（工人，军人，商人）。

Exercise 3

Fill in the brackets with the appropriate characters so as
to give the hanzi equivalent of the English.

1) farmer 　（　　　　）民

2) factory worker （　　　　　）人

3) policeman （　　　　）察

4) businessman 　（　　　　　）人

5) soldier 　（　　　　　）人

6) civil servant 公（　　　　）员

Lesson 13

Lesson 14 ~ *Common surnames*

*L*et's look at the characters for some of the commonest
surnames used in China.

李	Lǐ	
王	Wáng	*also means 'king'*
张	Zhāng	*also used for the measure word 'piece'*
刘	Liú	
陈	Chén	
杨	Yáng	
黄	Huáng	*also means 'yellow'*

Chinese typically adds 老 or 小 (lǎo or xiǎo) in front
of the surname meaning 'old' or 'little' respectively.
For example, 小王 means 'little Wang' and 老李
means 'old Li'. Use this when talking to or about
friends or colleagues.

New hanzi

先 生	Xiān shēng	Mr, sir	王先生	(Mr Wang)
女 士	Nǚ shì	Ms, lady	张女士	(Ms Zhang)

In Chinese you say Wang Mr not Mr Wang.

Exercise 1

Underline the character in each group which is not one of the surnames given above.

1) 丰　王　李　　4) 扬　张　王

2) 季　刘　张　　5) 张　王　引

3) 黄　阵　杨

Exercise 2

Rearrange these jumbled captions.

Mr Wang

Mr Chen

1) 陈先生

2) 刘女士

. . . .

. . . .

Ms Li

Ms Liu

3) 王先生

4) 李女士

. . . .

. . . .

Lesson 14

Exercise 3

Fill in the missing characters in the brackets so as to complete each sentence. Say each Chinese sentence out loud when you have done this.

1) Mr Liu is a policeman.

（　　　　　）是一位（　　　　　）。

2) Ms Wang is a civil servant.

（　　　　　）是一位（　　　　　）。

3) Old Chen is a factory worker.

（　　　　　）是一位（　　　　　）。

4) Little Li is reading.

（　　　　　）在看书。

5) Please sit down, Ms Yang.

请坐，（　　　　　）。

6) When did teacher Zhang leave?

张（　　　　　）什么（　　　　　）走的？

7) Good morning, Ms Li.

（　　　　　），李女士。

8) See you tomorrow, doctor Zhang.

明天见,（　　　　　）。

9) Where's old Huang?

（　　　　　）在哪里?

There are several characters pronounced yang (but with different tones). Can you identify the one that is the surname?

Puzzle

1) 扬

4) 炀　　　2) 杨

3) 样

Lesson 15 ~ *Some more surnames*

In this lesson we're going to learn the characters for some more commonly used Chinese surnames.

赵	Zhào	孙	Sūn
周	Zhōu	朱	Zhū
吴	Wú	马	Mǎ
徐	Xú		

Exercise 1

Identify the character in each group which is not one of the surnames listed above.

1) 马　赶　周

2) 昊　孙　吴

3) 徐　未　孙

4) 冯　周　赵

5) 马　涂　朱

Exercise 2

Rearrange the following captions.

Mr Zhu

Mr Wu

1) 孙女士

2) 马女士

Ms Sun

Ms Ma

3) 吴先生

4) 朱先生

Exercise 3

Fill in the missing characters in the brackets so as to make each sentence complete. Say each Chinese sentence out loud when you have done this.

1) Where are you going, old Zhou?

你去（　　　　），老（　　　　）？

2) Hello Ms Xu, I'm little Chen.

你好，（　　　　），我是小陈。

3) This is not Mr Ma's book.

这不是（　　　　）的（　　　　）。

Lesson 15

4) She is doctor Wu's daughter.

她是（   ）的女儿。

5) Mr Sun is not at home.

（   ）不在家。

6) Is old Zhu a factory worker?

（   ）是一位工人吗？

7) Is Mr Zhao a businessman?

（   ）是一位商人吗？

Lesson 16 ~ *Countries*

*N*ow we're going to learn some characters for countries.

中 国 Zhōng guó

英 国 Yīng guó

美 国 Měi guó

法 国 Fǎ guó

德 国 Dé guó

意 大 利 Yì dà lì

西 班 牙 Xī bān yá

日 本 Rì běn

Remember the following phrases:

你从哪里来？ 我从…来。	Nǐ cóng nǎ lǐ lái? Wǒ cóng…lái.	Where are you from? I'm from…

When talking about nationalities (eg I am American, she is an American), we add the hanzi 人 after the country name. For example:

英国人 美国人 中国人	Brit, British American Chinese (person)

Let's do some exercises.

Exercise 1

Rearrange the following captions.

1) 中国   2) 西班牙   3) 法国   4) 英国

5) 日本   6) 意大利   7) 美国

Exercise 2

Write out the correct translation from the three options given.

1) She is from the UK. （她从法国来，
她从英国来， 她从美国来）

· ·

2) He is Chinese.　（他是英国人，
他是法国人，他是中国人）

. . . .

3) My older sister is in America.

（我姐姐在西班牙，我姐姐是美国人，
我姐姐在美国）

. . . .

4) Her dad is French.　（她爸爸是德国人，
她爸爸是美国人，她爸爸是法国人）

. . . .

5) I'm not Japanese, I'm Chinese.

（我不是从日本来，我是从德国来；
我是日本人，不是中国人；
我不是日本人，是中国人）

. . . .

Lesson 16

Lesson 16

Exercise 3

Complete these translations by filling in the missing hanzi. Say your answers out loud.

1) Hello, I'm old Wang. I'm from China.

你好，我是（　　　　　）。

我从（　　　　　）来。

2) He's a German policeman.

他是一位（　　　　　）警察。

3) Mr Zhou is going to Japan next year.

周先生明年去（　　　　　）。

4) My younger brother is going to Italy next Monday.

我弟弟下（　　　　）去（　　　　　）。

5) Where are you from? I'm from Spain.

你从（　　　　）来？

我从（　　　　）来。

The character 中 zhōng is a useful one. It means 'middle' and is also a short form for 'China'. 中国 is the Middle Kingdom – in the days of the Chinese Empire the Chinese saw China as the centre of the world.

Block 4

Quiz

1. 一月有三十天。
    True or false?

2. Which of these is likely to chase a 猫? Is it
    a) 猪   **b)** 鸭   **c)** 狗?

3. Which country's flag has these colours: 红白蓝?
    a) 德国   **b)** 美国   **c)** 日本

4. 哪一个快？
    a) 汽车   **b)** 自行车   **c)** 飞机

5. 哪一个慢？
    a) 马   **b)** 猪   **c)** 虎

6. 我的手机不好。
    Why can't you contact your friends?

7. 那是你的老师...？
    Which character is missing in this question?

8. 她不喜欢他。
    Why wouldn't she be his girlfriend?

9. Who's most likely to cure an illness?
    a) 农民   **b)** 律师   **c)** 医生

10. 没有水在冰箱里。
    What's stopping you having a drink?

Lesson 1

Look closely at these signs.

tuī push

lā pull

Exercise 1

Now cover up the pictures and circle the correct hanzi for push and pull.

		a)	b)	c)	d)
1)	tuī push	锥	椎	雅	推
2)	lā pull	位	拉	立	往

Exercise 2

How many strokes do each of these hanzi have?

1) 拉

2) 推

Exercise 3

Little Bao Bao
comes up against

and gets stuck. Fill in the missing hanzi to complete what
Bao Bao's dad says to him.

爸爸说：是（　　），不是（　　）。

Lesson 2

New hanzi

rù kǒu entrance

chū kǒu exit

chū zhàn exit

Exercise 1

Can you identify which in each of the following groups is the hanzi for entrance/exit?

	a)	b)	c)
1)	人口	大口	入口
2)	山口	出口	小口
3)	出站	入站	人口

Exercise 2

Read these dialogues and then answer the questions.

女儿：妈妈，我要回家。
妈妈：好，出口在哪？
女儿：在那！

Which is the correct sign to point to?

a)

b)

c)

儿子：爸爸，入口在哪？
爸爸：看，在前边！

Which is the correct sign for the father to point to?

 d)

e)

f)

Exercise 3

Write down the correct hanzi to complete the following questions.

1) 对不起，rù kǒu 在哪?

. . . .

2) 对不起，chū kǒu 在哪?

. . . .

3) 对不起，从哪 chū zhàn?

. . . .

Lesson 2

Lesson 3

New hanzi

卫 生 间	wèi shēng jiān	toilet
洗 手 间	xǐ shǒu jiān	toilet

Exercise 1

Draw an arrow to the sign for toilets on this notice board.

Exercise 2

Here are two signs.

a)

b)

Now read this Chinese and then answer the questions below by putting in the picture number.

1) 我的妹妹要去卫生间。
妹妹去哪里? 妹妹去…

2) 她的弟弟要去卫生间。

弟弟去哪里? 弟弟去…

Clue: check Block 1 Lesson 13.

Exercise 3

One of the characters in this notice has disappeared. Can you supply the missing one? Is it:

a) 们

b) 问

c) 间

d) 闲

e) 简

Lesson 4

New hanzi

| 学校 | xué xiào | school |

Exercise 1

You have arranged to meet your friends at the primary school. Walking around you see three signs all containing the hanzi 学.

a)

b)

c)

Which one is the primary school?

Clue: check the hanzi for 'little' and 'big' in Block 3 Lesson 9.

Exercise 2

The same character can look very different when written in different styles. Write down the character, which you have learned so far, that appears both in the top line of this sign and on the banner below.

Exercise 3

If 小学 is primary school, can you work out what these signs are?

1)

2)

Clue: 中 is in Block 3 Lesson 16

Identify the correct Chinese translation for these sentences from the options given. Write your answers down, saying them out loud.

你的大学在哪？

他在上中学。

你的小学在哪？

1) Where is your primary school?

. . . .

2) Where is your university?

. . . .

3) He's at secondary school.

. . . .

Lesson 4

Lesson 5

New hanzi

医 院	yī yuàn	hospital
挂 号	guà hào	to register
收 费	shōu fèi	payment
药 房	yào fáng	dispensary
急 诊	jí zhěn	emergency

Exercise 1

Where does the ambulance go?

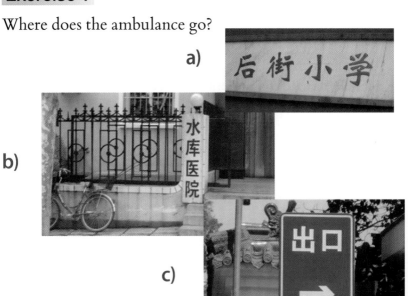

a)

b)

c)

Exercise 2

Choose the correct picture on the page opposite to answer each of these questions.

1) If there is an emergency, where should a patient go?

. . . .

2) Where does a patient go to pay his bill?

. . . .

3) Where does a patient go to pick up his medicine?

. . . .

4) Where does a patient go to register?

. . . .

a)

b)

c)

d)

Lesson 6

New hanzi

银 行	yín háng	bank
公 用 电 话	gōng yòng diàn huà	public phone
地 铁	dì tiě	underground
网 吧	wǎng bā	internet café

Look at these pictures.

a)

b)

c)

d)

Exercise 1

Match each Chinese sentence with the appropriate photo.

1) 对不起，公用电话在哪？ . . . .

2) 我妈妈星期一要去银行。 . . . .

3) 他哥哥明天想去网吧。 . . . .

4) 地铁站在东边。 . . . .

Lesson 6

Exercise 2

Read this Chinese sentence and then enter the correct sequence of the places that were visited.

星期四下午我坐地铁去银行，然后用公用电话给我姐姐打了一个电话，最后去了网吧。

Is it **a) b)** or **c)**?

a) abdc

b) cabd

c) dabc

New Hanzi

然后	rán hòu	then
最后	zuì hòu	finally

Lesson 7

*I*n Chinese there is no one word for restaurant. But there are several key hanzi which you will see and which are used in signs for restaurants. Here are some of them.

New hanzi

餐	cān	meals
吃	chī	to eat
饭	fàn	rice
酒	jiǔ	wine
面	miàn	noodles

Exercise 1

In each of these pictures draw an arrow to the hanzi which suggests to you that this is a restaurant.

1)

2)

3)

4)

5)

饺子王　手擀面

6)

中华老字号
隆福寺小吃店
隆福寺餐饮公司

Lesson 7

Exercise 2

Look at the top line of this sign. What sort of food will you get here?

Clue: Block 3 Lesson 7.

Exercise 3

When Bao Bao came out of primary school his parents took him to the supermarket to do some shopping. Bao Bao then needed the toilet. Then they went to a restaurant for dinner. Put the following photos in the correct sequence to describe what they did.

a)

b)

c)

d)

Answers

Block 1

Lesson 1

1 1) 大   2) 人   3) 回   4) 丰   5) 力

2 1) 一二三四 yī èr sān sì   2) 三五七九 sān wǔ qī jiǔ
   3) 二五七十 èr wǔ qī shí   4) 三六八九 sān liù bā jiǔ
   5) 一四九十 yī sì jiǔ shí

3 1) 十八二一 shí bā èr yī   2) 九四三一 jiǔ sì sān yī
   3) 十七六五 shí qī liù wǔ   4) 八七三二 bā qī sān èr
   5) 九六五一 jiǔ liù wǔ yī

4 1) 四   2) 五   3) 七   4) 八   5) 九

5 1) 六 liù   2) 九 jiǔ   3) 三 sān   4) 四 sì   5) 十 shí

6 1) 二 èr   2) 九 jiǔ   3) 四 sì   4) 一 yī   5) 六 liù

Lesson 2

1 1) 七；èr jiā wǔ děng yú qī   2) 八；qī jiā yī děng yú bā
   3) 七；sān jiā sì děng yú qī   4) 四；shí jiǎn liù děng yú sì
   5) 六；bā jiǎn èr děng yú liù

2 1) 太   2) 丰   3) 为   4) 木   5) 丸

3 1) 七；sì jiā sān děng yú qī   2) 八；liù jiā èr děng yú bā
   3) 十；yī jiā jiǔ děng yú shí   4) 五；èr jiā sān děng yú wǔ
   5) 九；sì jiā wǔ děng yú jiǔ

4 1) 九；shí jiǎn yī děng yú jiǔ   2) 四；qī jiǎn sān děng yú sì
   3) 三；liù jiǎn sān děng yú sān   4) 二；shí jiǎn bā děng yú èr
   5) 五；bā jiǎn sān děng yú wǔ

5 1) 七；èr jiā liù jiǎn yī děng yú qī
   2) 五；qī jiā èr jiǎn sì děng yú wǔ
   3) 二；sì jiā wǔ jiǎn qī děng yú èr
   4) 八；sān jiā liù jiǎn yī děng yú bā
   5) 九；liù jiā sì jiǎn yī děng yú jiǔ

Lesson 3

1   1) 四十 sì shí   2) 五十 wǔ shí   3) 六十 liù shí
    4) 七十 qī shí   5) 八十 bā shí   6) 八十五 bā shí wǔ
    7) 九十 jiǔ shí

2   1) 十五；sān chéng yǐ wǔ děng yú shí wǔ
    2) 十八；èr chéng yǐ jiǔ děng yú shí bā
    3) 四十；sì chéng yǐ shí děng yú sì shí
    4) 七十二；bā chéng yǐ jiǔ děng yú qī shí èr
    5) 三；liù chú yǐ èr děng yú sān
    6) 四；shí èr chú yǐ sān děng yú sì
    7) 十一；èr shí èr chú yǐ èr děng yú shí yī
    8) 七；wǔ shí liù chú yǐ bā děng yú qī

3   1) 十二   2) 三十   3) 四十五   4) 六十六
    5) 八十   6) 七十五   7) 七十二   8) 八十六

4   1) 三   2) 五   3) 二   4) 九   5) 十五
    6) 六   7) 二十五   8) 八

Puzzle

Lesson 4

1   1) 二百三十五   2) 一百九十六   3) 四百六十
    4) 二百   5) 五百零三   6) 二百零三

2   1) 白   2) 方   3) 干   4) 乙   5) 于   6) 力

3   1) 二百一十四   2) 一千九百五十六
    3) 七万八千一百六十三   4) 二百七十八万四千五百
    5) 九千三百二十四   6) 十万八千

Lesson 5

1   1) 在 西边 zài xī biān   2) 在东边 zài dōng biān
    3) 在南边 zài nán biān   4) 在东北 zài dōng běi
    5) 在西北 zài xī běi   6) 在东南 zài dōng nán
    7) 在西南 zài xī nán

2   **1)** supermarket   **2)** hotel   **3)** gym
    4) park   **5)** airport   **6)** restaurant

Lesson 6

1   **1)** 上   **2)** 左边   **3)** 上   **4)** 下   **5)** 上   **6)** 左边   **7)** 右边
2   **1)** 卞   **2)** 土   **3)** 石
3   **1)** 左 zuǒ   **2)** 上 shàng   **3)** 东 dōng   **4)** 边 biān
    5) 在 zài   **6)** 右 yòu   **7)** 西 xī

Lesson 7

1   **1)** 里边   **2)** 上   **3)** 外边   **4)** 后边   **5)** 前边
    6) 里边   **7)** 左边   **8)** 右边   **9)** 后边   **10)** 外边
    11) 里边
2   **1)** 里 lǐ   **2)** 边 biān   **3)** 后 hòu   **4)** 南 nán
    5) 北 běi   **6)** 在 zài   **7)** 外 wài   **8)** 前 qián
3   **1)** 西 xī   **2)** 前 qián   **3)** 里 lǐ   **4)** 右 yòu   **5)** 南 nán

Lesson 8

1   **1)** 买   **2)** 于   **3)** 必   **4)** 北   **5)** 是
2   **1)** 头   **2)** 背   **3)** 心   **4)** 脚   **5)** 手

Lesson 9

1   **1)** 右   **2)** 聂   **3)** 芽   **4)** 月   **5)** 古
2   **1)** 下巴   **2)** 舌   **3)** 耳   **4)** 牙   **5)** 脸   **6)** 发头
3   **1)** tóu   **2)** ěr   **3)** shǒu   **4)** jiǎo   **5)** tóu fà   **6)** yá   **7)** xīn

Lesson 10

1   **1)** 九点   **2)** 十二点   **3)** 三点二十五
    4) 五点四十   **5)** 六点三十（六点半）
2   **1)** 三点十六（分）   **2)** 五点四十三（分）
    3) 十二点四十八（分）   **4)** 七点五十九（分）   **5)** 九点半
3   **1)** 两小时   **2)** 三小时四十分
    3) 两小时三十分   **4)** 四小时三十分

Lesson 11

Puzzle   The two characters are 上 and 下.

1 **1)** 下牛   **2)** 卜午   **3)** 申午   **4)** 下干   **5)** 土午

2 **1)** 早上六点 zǎo shàng liù diǎn

2) 中午十二点 zhōng wǔ shí èr diǎn

3) 下午五点二十五 xià wǔ wǔ diǎn èr shí wǔ

4) 下午三点四十 xià wǔ sān diǎn sì shí

5) 下午四点三十（下午四点半）xià wǔ sì diǎn sān shí (xià wǔ sì diǎn bàn)

6) 晚上八点 wǎn shàng bā diǎn

3 **1)** 下午三点十六分   **2)** 下午五点四十三分

3) 中午十二点十分   **4)** 早上七点五十九分

5) 上午九点半

Lesson 12

1 **1)** 夫   **2)** 四   **3)** 用   **4)** 田

2 **1)** 周一   **2)** 星期二   **3)** 周三   **4)** 星期四

5) 周五   **6)** 周六   **7)** 星期日

3 **1)** 周日上午   **2)** 周四中午

3) 周六下午   **4)** 周二下午一点半

5) 周五下午四点四十   **6)** 周日中午十二点

Lesson 13

1 **1)** 力   **2)** 田   **3)** 安   **4)** 入   **5)** 了   **6)** 好

2 **1)** 男人   **2)** 老人   **3)** 女人   **4)** 孩子

3 **1)** 一个老人 yí gè lǎo rén

2) 十个女人 shí gè nǚ rén

3) 一百三十七个人 yì bǎi sān shí qī gè rén

4) 四十个男人 sì shí gè nán rén

5) 十五个孩子 shí wǔ gè hái zi

Lesson 14

1 1) 祖母   2) 祖父   3) 孙女   4) 母亲

2 1) 租   2) 爻   3) 儿   4) 了

3 1) 祖父；George shì Jimmy de zǔ fù.
   2) 祖母；Sheila shì Peter de zǔ mǔ.
   3) 儿子；Jack shì Hilda de ér zi.
   4) 孙子；Jimmy shì George de sūn zi.
   5) 母亲；Hilda shì Jack de mǔ qīn.
   6) 女儿；Jane shì Tom de nǔ ér.

Puzzle   mǔ qīn jié is Mother's Day

Lesson 15

1 1) 周三   2) 周二   3) 周四   4) 周五

2 1) 今天下午两点 jīn tiān xià wǔ liǎng diǎn
   2) 昨天上午八点 zuó tiān shàng wǔ bā diǎn
   3) 明天是周三。 Míng tiān shì zhōu sān.
   4) 后天是周日。 Hòu tiān shì zhōu rì.
   5) 周六下午两点 zhōu liù xià wǔ liǎng diǎn
   6) 周二上午十点四十 zhōu èr shàng wǔ shí diǎn sì shí

Lesson 16

1 1) 十二；yī nián yǒu shí èr gè yuè
   2) 六十；yī xiǎo shí yǒu liù shí fēn
   3) 三十；bàn xiǎo shí yǒu sān shí fēn
   4) 二十四；yī tiān yǒu èr shí sì gè xiǎo shí

2 1) 一九九八年七月五日 yī jiǔ jiǔ bā nián qī yuè wǔ rì
   2) 去年十二月 qù nián shí èr yuè
   3) 明年一月 míng nián yī yuè
   4) 下周一 xià zhōu yī
   5) 今年九月十八日 jīn nián jiǔ yuè shí bā rì
   6) 去年四月十三日 qù nián sì yuè shí sān rì

3 1) 五月十日 wǔ yuè shí rì   2) 五月十二日 wǔ yuè shí èr rì
   3) 周日 zhōu rì   4) 早上七点 zǎo shàng qī diǎn

5) 早上八点十分 zǎo shàng bā diǎn shí fēn
6) 早上八点 zǎo shàng bā diǎn
7) 下午三点四十五 xià wǔ sān diǎn sì shí wǔ
8) 周六 zhōu liù
9) 下午四点 xià wǔ sì diǎn
10) 五月十二日 wǔ yuè shí èr rì
11) Jane的祖母 Jane de zǔ mǔ

Lesson 17

1　1) 好　　　2) 笆　　　3) 斧　　　4) 乃
2　1) 爸爸　　2) 妈妈　　3) 爷爷　　4) 奶奶
3　1) 爷爷；George shì Jimmy de yé ye.
　　2) 爸爸；Tom shì Jane de bà ba.
　　3) 奶奶；Sheila shì Peter de nǎi nai.
　　4) 妈妈；Hilda shì Jack de mā ma.

Lesson 18

1　1) 歌　　　2) 如　　　3) 第　　　4) 昧
2　1) 哥哥　　2) 姐姐　　3) 弟弟　　4) 妹妹
3　1) 妹妹；Mandy shì Bob de mèi mei.
　　2) 哥哥；Bob shì Mandy de gē ge.
　　3) 姐姐；Amy shì Bob de jiě jie.
　　4) 弟弟；Bob shì Amy de dì di.

Lesson 19

1　1) 耳　　　2) 用　　　3) 元　　　4) 凤　　　5) 需
2　1) 山　　　2) 云　　　3) 月　　　4) 雨

Lesson 20

1　1) 王　　2) 本　　3) 何　　4) 永　　5) 伙　　6) 士
2　1) 河　　2) 火　　3) 土　　4) 木
4　1) 光　guāng　　　2) 舌　shé　　　3) 男　nán
　　4) 月　yuè　　　5) 哥　gē

Block 2

Quiz

1. 21 **2.** 80 **3.** True **4.** Thursday **5.** True **6.** False
7. False **8.** 手 **9.** 妹妹 **10.** It goes out.

Lesson 1

1 1) 地   2) 找   3) 奶   4) 宅

2 1) he   2) I   3) she   4) it   5) you

3 1) 它在里边。 Tā zài lǐ biān.   2) 你是哥哥。 Nǐ shì gē ge.
   3) 我是妹妹。 Wǒ shì mèi mei. 4) 她是姐姐。 Tā shì jiě jie.
   5) 我是弟弟。 Wǒ shì dì di.   6) 他是爸爸。 Tā shì bà ba.
   7) 她是妈妈。 Tā shì mā ma.   8) 他是爷爷。 Tā shì yé ye.
   9) 她是奶奶。 Tā shì nǎi nai.

Lesson 2

Word combinations

来回 lái huí   回来 huí lái   坐下 zuò xià
回去 huí qù   走回去 zǒu huí qù

1 1) 未   2) 座   3) 水   4) 故   5) 徒

2 1) to return   2) to come   3) to go
   4) to do   5) to walk   6) to sit

3 1) 爸爸回去了。   2) 他坐下了。   3) 她昨天走了。
   4) 我今天上午八点四十来了。 5) 妈妈昨天下午回来了。

Lesson 3

1 1) 着   2) 军   3) 悦   4) 笋   5) 间

2 1) 看   2) 笑   3) 哭   4) 说   5) 写   6) 问

3 1) 妹妹哭了。 2) 我昨天做了。 3) 我前天看了。 4) 他写了。

Lesson 4

1 1) to go home   2) to read a book   3) to work
   4) to write   5) to write a book   6) to speak

2 **1)** 我在写字。   **2)** 爸爸在看书。 **3)** 妈妈在说话。
4) 爷爷在写书。   **5)** 她回家了。
6) 奶奶明天下午三点见我。   **7)** 我看见她在看书。

Lesson 5

1 **1)** 什么   **2)** 什么时候   **3)** 为什么   **4)** 谁

2 **1)** why?   **2)** what?   **3)** who?   **4)** when?

3 **1)** 他昨天什么时候回家了?
Tā zuó tiān shén me shí hòu huí jiā le?

2) 她为什么在哭? Tā wèi shén me zài kū?

3) 妈妈说什么了? Mā ma shuō shén me le?

4) 谁在说话? Shéi zài shuō huà?

5) 你问谁了? Nǐ wèn shéi le?

6) 你在看什么? Nǐ zài kàn shén me?

4 **1)** 什么时候 Nǐ shén me shí hòu huí jiā le?

2) 什么 Nǐ zuó tiān xià wǔ zuò shén me le?

3) 什么 Tā zài zuò shén me?

4) 谁 Shéi zài shuō huà?

5 **1)** 谁   **2)** 她   **3)** 我

Lesson 6

1 **1)** 从   **2)** 和   **3)** 正在   **4)** 已经

2 **1)** already   **2)** *continuous tense indicator*
3) and   **4)** from

3 **1)** 他和她。   Tā hé tā.

2) 你和我。   Nǐ hé wǒ.

3) 妈妈和爸爸。   Mā ma hé bà ba.

4) 他从英国来。   Tā cóng Yīng guó lái.

5) 我从上海来。   Wǒ cóng Shànghǎi lái.

6) 她正在看书。   Tā zhèng zài kàn shū.

7) 他已经走了。　Tā yǐ jīng zǒu le.

8) 我已经做了。　Wǒ yǐ jīng zuò le.

Lesson 7

1　**1)** us　　　**2)** they *(female)*　　　**3)** they　　　**4)** you

2　**1)** 他们已经走了。　Tā men yǐ jīng zǒu le.

2) 我们正在说话。　Wǒ men zhèng zài shuō huà.

3) 你们为什么在笑？　Nǐ men wèi shén me zài xiào?

4) 他们已经走了。　Tā men yǐ jīng zǒu le.

5) 她们在哭。　Tā men zài kū.

Lesson 8

1　**1)** its tā de　　　**2)** their tā men de　　　**3)** your nǐ de
　　4) ours wǒ men de　　**5)** her tā de

2　**1)** 他是我的爷爷。　Tā shì wǒ de yé ye.

2) 她是他的姐姐。　Tā shì tā de jiě jie.

3) 他们是我的妈妈和爸爸。
Tā men shì wǒ de mā ma hé bà ba.

4) 它是你的。　Tā shì nǐ de.

5) 他的弟弟正在看书。　Tā de dì di zhèng zài kàn shū.

3　**1)** my hand(s)　　　**2)** our younger sisters　　　**3)** her hair
　　4) their parents　　**5)** your children

Lesson 9

1　**1)** nà xiē　　　**2)** zhè lǐ　　　**3)** zhè xiē
　　4) zhè ge　　　**5)** nà lǐ　　　**6)** zhè

2　**1)** 这是我的爸爸。　Zhè shì wǒ de bà ba.

2) 那是谁？　Nà shì shéi.

3) 我在这里。　Wǒ zài zhè lǐ.

4) 他坐在那里。　Tā zuò zài nà lǐ.

5) 这些人昨天走了。　Zhè xiē rén zuó tiān zǒu le.

6) 那些人已经来了。 Nà xiē rén yǐ jīng lái le.

7) 这个人在看书。 Zhè ge rén zài kàn shū.

3 **1)** Zhè shì wǒ de fù mǔ. These are my parents.

2) Nà shì tā men de. That is theirs.

3) Zhè xiē shì wǒ men de. These are ours.

4) Nǐ de zài zhè lǐ. Yours is (are) here.

5) Tā men de zài nà lǐ. Theirs is (are) there.

Lesson 10

1 **1)** 本 liǎng běn shū   **2)** 个 sān gè rén

3) 杯 liǎng bēi shuǐ   **4)** 支 yì zhī bǐ

5) 张 yì zhāng zhǐ   **6)** 块 sān kuài shí tou

7) 只 wǔ zhī niǎo

2 **1)** 只   **2)** 块   **3)** 支   **4)** 本   **5)** 杯

3 **1)** I have three books. Wǒ yǒu sān běn shū.

2) My older sister has two sons. Wǒ de jiě jie yǒu liǎng gè ér zi.

3) There's a glass of water over there. Nà lǐ yǒu yì bēi shuǐ.

4) Here are three pens. Zhè lǐ yǒu sān zhī bǐ.

5) He's writing on a piece of paper. Tā zài yì zhāng zhǐ shàng xiě zì.

Lesson 11

1 **1)** where?   **2)** how?   **3)** whose?   **4)** how many?

2 **1)** 你有多少本书? Nǐ yǒu duō shǎo běn shū?

2) 他昨天去哪里了? Tā zuó tiān qù ná lǐ le?

3) 那是谁的笔? Nà shì shéi de bǐ?

4) 你有多少个孩子? Nǐ yǒu duō shǎo gè hái zi?

5) 他怎么了? Tā zěn me le?

6) 她多大了? Tā duó dà le?

3 **1)** 什么, 我, 看书   **2)** 多大, 15 or 十五

3) 昨天, 哪里, 去上海了   **4)** 谁的, 你妈妈

Lesson 12

1 **1)** few **2)** many **3)** beautiful **4)** bad **5)** good **6)** ugly

2 **1)** 多 duō **2)** 美 měi **3)** 坏 huài **4)** 笑 xiào **5)** 来 lái

3 **1)** 我的妹妹说我是她的好姐姐。

  2) 我有一个坏消息。 **3)** 他有很多孩子。

  4) 那边的人少。 **5)** 这个人很丑。

Lesson 13

1 **1)** short **2)** wrong **3)** hot **4)** long **5)** right **6)** cold

2 **1)** 那 nà **2)** 短 duǎn **3)** 热 rè **4)** 错 cuò

  5) 少 shǎo **6)** 丑 chǒu **7)** 好 hǎo

3 **1)** 她做对了。 **2)** 他说他错了。 **3)** 今天很冷。

  4) 一杯热水 **5)** 我有长头发。

Lesson 14

1 **1)** extremely **2)** very **3)** fairly **4)** particularly **5)** too

2 **1)** 今天太热了。 **2)** 这个比较长。 **3)** 有个很坏的消息。

  4) 她非常美。 **5)** 去年十二月特别冷。

Puzzle **3)** 很

Lesson 15

1 **1)** both **2)** to **3)** also **4)** not **5)** no **6)** again

2 **1)** 她在对我笑。 Tā zài duì wǒ xiào.

  2) 妈妈又回来了。

  3) 这个也很好。 Zhè ge yě hěn hǎo.

  4) 今天不冷。

  5) 我没问她。 Wǒ méi wèn tā.

  6) 爷爷和奶奶都不来了。 Yé ye hé nǎi nai dōu bù lái le.

Puzzle **5)** 没

Lesson 16

1 1) 是, 不是　　　　2) 是，吗, 不是, 是　　　　3) 有, 没有

2 1) 她不是我（的）妹妹。　她是我（的）姐姐。　Tā bú shì wǒ (de) mèi mei. Tā shì wǒ (de) jiě jie.

2) 我（的）爷爷没（有）在看书。他在写字。　Wǒ (de) yé ye méi (yǒu) zài kàn shū. Tā zài xiě zì.

3) 他昨天回来了吗？ Tā zuó tiān huí lái le ma?

4) 我没有那本书。　Wǒ méi yǒu nà běn shū.

Lesson 17

1 1) 要 or 想要　2) 得 or 要　　　　3) 会 or 能
4) 会　　　5) 想 or 想要 or 要　6) 请
7) 不能　　　8) 不 or 不会

2 1) 他想（要）看书, 不想说话。　Tā xiǎng (yào) kàn shū, bù xiǎng shuō huà.

2) 我姐姐明天想见我。　Wǒ jiě jie míng tiān xiǎng jiàn wǒ.

3) 他明天不会来了。　Tā míng tiān bú huì lái le.

4) 你明天不能回家。　Nǐ míng tiān bù néng huí jiā.

5) 我请她来这里。　Wǒ qǐng tā lái zhè lǐ.

Lesson 18

1 1) 不知道　　　2) 可以　　　3) 不能（不可以）
4) 必须（应该）　5) 需要　　　6) 不应该

2 1) 我不知道你是谁。　Wǒ bù zhī dào nǐ shì shéi.

2) 你不可以明天来这里。　Nǐ bù kě yǐ míng tiān lái zhè lǐ.

3) 你必须在下午两点回家。　Nǐ bì xū zài xià wǔ liǎng diǎn huí jiā.

4) 她应该在这里见我。

5) 我不知道她需要多少本书。　Wǒ bù zhī dào tā xū yào duō shǎo běn shū.

Lesson 19

1　1) good morning　　2) hello　　　　3) good night
　　4) bye-bye　　　　 5) good evening　6) see you later

2　1) 我们应该在早上说 "早上好"。
　　2) 我们应该在下午说 "下午好"。
　　3) 我们应该在晚上说 "晚上好"。
　　4) 她对我说 "回头见"。
　　5) 他妈妈对他说 "晚安"。

3　1) wǎn ān 晚安　　　2) nǐ hǎo 你好
　　3) zài jiàn 再见　　 4) zǎo shàng hǎo 早上好

Lesson 20

1　1) méi guān xi　2) duì bù qǐ　　　3) láo jià
　　4) xiè xiè　　　 5) duō bǎo zhòng

2　1)　A：对不起　　A: Duì bù qǐ.
　　　 B：没关系　　B: Méi guān xi.

　　2) 非常感谢　Tā shuō, "Nǐ tài hǎo le! Fēi cháng gǎn xiè!"
　　　 不客气 Wǒ shuō, "Bú kè qi."

　　3)　B：没问题
　　　　 A: Wǒ xiǎng yào yì bēi shuǐ.
　　　　 B: Méi wèn tí.

　　4)　A：劳驾　Láo jià, zhè ge shì wǒ de, nà ge shì nǐ de.

　　5)　A：劳驾　Láo jià, jǐ diǎn le?

　　6)　B：多保重
　　　　 A: Míng tiān jiàn.
　　　　 B: Hǎo de. Duō bǎo zhòng.

Block 3

Quiz

1. b) 他　**2. b)** 做　**3. c)** huí　**4.** 问　**5. b)** 回家　**6. c)** 明年一月　**7. a)** 为什么?　**8.** 她们 should be 他们　**9. b)** 本 běn　**10. c)** 丑 chǒu

Lesson 1

1　**1)** 袜子　　**2)** 上衣　　**3)** 手套　　**4)** 大衣　　**5)** 鞋子

2　**1)** 双　sān shuāng xié zi　　**2)** 件　yí jiàn dà yī

　　3) 双　liǎng shuāng shǒu tào　　**4)** 个　liù gè rén

　　5) 条　sì tiáo kù zi

3　**1)** I have two pairs of gloves. Wǒ yǒu liǎng shuāng shǒu tào.

　　2) This is my older sister's coat, not mine. Zhè shì wǒ jiě jie de dà yī, bú shì wǒ de.

　　3) Whose shoes are these? Zhè shì shéi de xié zi?

　　4) This pair of trousers is very long. Zhè tiáo kù zi hěn cháng.

　　5) Where are my socks? Wǒ de wà zi zài nǎ lǐ?

Lesson 2

1　**1)** 紫色　purple　　**2)** 黄色　yellow　　**3)** 粉色　pink

　　4) 白色　white　　**5)** 红色　red　　**6)** 绿色　green

　　7) 黑色　black　　**8)** 蓝色　blue

2　**1)** 黑色　hēi sè　　**2)** 紫色　zǐ sè　　**3)** 黄色　huáng sè

　　4) 白色　bái sè　　**5)** 蓝色　lán sè　　**6)** 绿色　lǜ sè

　　7) 红色　hóng sè　　**8)** 粉色　fěn sè

3　**1)** 蓝色；黄色　Wǒ yǒu yì shuāng lán sè de shǒu tào, wǒ mèi mei yǒu yì shuāng huáng sè de.

2) 白色　Wǒ de shàng yī shì bái sè de.

3) 没；红色　Wǒ méi kàn jiàn tā nà shuāng hóng sè de xié zi.

4) 粉色　Wǒ xiǎng yào nà jiàn fěn sè de.

Lesson 3

1　**1)** 桃子　peach　**2)** 苹果　apple　**3)** 草　grass
　4) 树　tree　**5)** 水果　fruit　**6)** 梨　pear
　7) 花　flower　**8)** 香蕉　banana

2　**1)** 三个梨　three pears　sān gè lí

　2) 红色的苹果　red apples　hóng sè de píng guǒ

　3) 很多紫色的花　a lot of purple flowers　hěn duō zǐ sè de huā

　4) 一些桔子　some oranges　yì xiē jú zi

　5) 你喜欢什么水果?　What fruit do you like?　Nǐ xǐ huān shén me shuǐ guǒ?

　6) 我喜欢香蕉。　I like bananas.　Wǒ xǐ huān xiāng jiāo.

　7) 我的爸爸不喜欢桃子。　My dad doesn't like peaches. Wǒ de bà ba bù xǐ huān táo zi.

　8) 那里有一些花。　There are some flowers.　Nà lǐ yǒu yì xiē huā.

Puzzle　**3)** 花

Lesson 4

1　**1)** 春天　**2)** 冬天　**3)** 下雨　**4)** 夏天

2　**1)** 夏天　**2)** 秋天　**3)** 冬天　**4)** 春天　**5)** 夏天

3　**1)** 来　**2)** 下　**3)** 冬, 夏　**4)** 喜欢　**5)** 在

Lesson 5

1　**1)** 杯子　bēi zi　**2)** 筷子　kuài zi　**3)** 刀　dāo
　4) 盘子　pán zi　**5)** 碟子　dié zi　**6)** 碗　wǎn
　7) 叉　chā

2 1) 个   2) 个   3) 把   4) 双   5) 把

3 1) 两个黄色的碗   2) 一双绿色的筷子
   3) 两个蓝色的盘子   4) 一个红色的碟子

Lesson 6

1 1) 红色的地毯 hóng sè de dì tǎn
   2) 黄色的桌子 huáng sè de zhuō zi
   3) 绿色的窗户 lǜ sè de chuāng hu
   4) 黑色的门 hēi sè de men
   5) 黄色的椅子 huáng sè de yǐ zi

2 1) on the table   2) Sit on the chair.
   3) in the cupboard   4) on the floor

Puzzle   5) 门

Lesson 7

1 1) 鸭   2) 鹅   3) 鸟   4) 天鹅   5) 鸡

2 鸟

3 1) There are two birds in the tree.   2) He saw a crow yesterday.
   3) I like white swans.   4) There are three chickens.

Lesson 8

1 1) 狗   2) 猪   3) 猫
   4) 虎   5) 狼   6) 猴

2 1) 只, 狗   2) 头, 牛   3) 只, 羊   4) 匹, 马

3 1) Zhè shì shéi de māo? Zhè shì wǒ de. Whose cat is this? It's mine.
   2) Wǒ yǒu yì zhī hēi sè de gǒu. I have a black dog.
   3) Nà bú shì wǒ de mǎ. That isn't my horse.
   4) Tā yǒu jǐ zhī yáng? Tā yǒu èr shí sì zhī yáng.
   How many sheep does he have? He has 24 sheep.

Lesson 9

1 1) 船 2) 公共汽车 3) 自行车
   4) 卡车 5) 汽车 6) 飞机

2 1) His older brother works on the buses.
   他的哥哥在公共汽车上工作。
   Tā de gē ge zài gōng gòng qì chē shàng gōng zuò.
   2) I don't have a bike. 我没有自行车。
   Wǒ méi yǒu zì xíng chē.
   3) I want a job working on a boat. 我想在船上工作。
   Wǒ xiǎng zài chuán shàng gōng zuò.

3 1) 飞机 2) 汽车 3) 火车 4) 公共汽车 5) 船

Lesson 10

1 1) 手表 2) 电脑 3) 电视 4) 冰箱 5) 电话 6) 手机

2 1) 苹果在冰箱上。 Píng guǒ zài bīng xiāng shàng.
   2) 我的电脑是黑色的。 Wǒ de diàn nǎo shì hēi sè de.
   3) 你的手表在桌子上。 Nǐ de shǒu biǎo zài zhuō zi shàng.
   4) 我在看电视。 Wǒ zài kàn diàn shì.

3 1) What's that? That's a fridge. 什么；冰箱
   2) Is this your watch? No, that's not my watch. Mine is red.
   手表；不；不是；手表；红色
   3) Whose computer is this? My younger brother's. 谁；弟弟的
   4) I don't have a telephone at home. 电话

Lesson 11

1 1) 笔记本 2) 尺子 3) 笔 4) 课本 5) 橡皮
2 1) 两块橡皮 2) 一支笔 3) 三个笔记本 4) 一把尺子
3 1) 笔 2) 铅笔 3) 她；课本
   4) 对不起；笔记本；哪 5) 纸；哪

274

Lesson 12

1 **1)** 法官   **2)** 学生   **3)** 老师   **4)** 律师   **5)** 护士

2 **1)** 一位老师   **2)** 三件大衣   **3)** 一个笔记本

 4) 两件上衣   **5)** 一双鞋子

3 **1)** 老师;医生   **2)** 护士   **3)** 法官

 4) 律师;晚上;什么时候   **5)** 三个学生

Lesson 13

1 **1)** 工人   **2)** 农民   **3)** 军人   **4)** 商人   **5)** 公务员

2 **1)** 警察   **2)** 商人   **3)** 公务员   **4)** 工人

3 **1)** 农   **2)** 工   **3)** 警   **4)** 商   **5)** 军   **6)** 务

Lesson 14

1 **1)** 丰   **2)** 季   **3)** 阵   **4)** 扬   **5)** 引

2 **1)** 王先生   **2)** 陈先生   **3)** 李女士   **4)** 刘女士

3 **1)** 刘先生;   警察 Liú xiān shēng shì yí wèi jǐng chá.

 2) 王女士;   公务员 Wáng nǔ shì shì yí wèi gōng wù yuán.

 3) 老陈;   工人 Lǎo Chén shì yí wèi gōng rén.

 4) 小李 Xiǎo Lǐ zài kàn shū.

 5) 杨女士 Qǐng zuò, Yáng nǔ shì.

 6) 老师;   时候 Zhāng lǎo shī shén me shí hòu zǒu de?

 7) 早上好 Zǎo shàng hǎo, Lǐ nǔ shì.

 8) 张医生 Míng tiān jiàn, Zhāng yī shēng.

 9) 老黄 Lǎo Huáng, zài nǎ lǐ?

Puzzle   **2)** 杨

Lesson 15

1 **1)** 赶   **2)** 昊   **3)** 未   **4)** 冯   **5)** 涂

2 **1)** 朱先生   **2)** 吴先生   **3)** 孙女士   **4)** 马女士

3 **1)** 哪里；周　Nǐ qù nǎ lǐ, lǎo Zhōu?

2) 徐女士　Nǐ hǎo, Xú nǚ shì, wǒ shì xiǎo Chén.

3) 马先生；书　Zhè bú shì Mǎ xiān shēng de shū.

4) 吴医生　Tā shì Wú yī shēng de nǚ ér.

5) 孙先生　Sūn xiān shēng bú zài jiā.

6) 老朱　Lǎo Zhū shì yí wèi gōng rén ma?

7) 赵先生　Zhào xiān shēng shì yí wèi shāng rén ma?

Lesson 16

1 **1)** 法国　　**2)** 英国　　**3)** 美国　　**4)** 意大利
5) 中国　　**6)** 西班牙　**7)** 日本

2 **1)** 她从英国来。　　**2)** 他是中国人。

3) 我姐姐在美国。　　**4)** 她爸爸是法国人。

5) 我不是日本人，是中国人。

3 **1)** 老王；中国　Nǐ hǎo. Wǒ shì lǎo Wáng. Wǒ cóng Zhōng guó lái.

2) 德国　Tā shì yí wèi Dé guó jǐng chá.

3) 日本　Zhōu xiān shēng míng nián huì qù Rì běn.

4) 星期一；意大利　Wǒ dì di xià xīng qī yī huì qù Yì dà lì.

5) 哪里；西班牙　Nǐ cóng nǎ lǐ lái? Wǒ cóng Xī bān yá lái.

Block 4

Quiz

1. False 2. c) 狗 3. b) 美国 4. c) 飞机 5. b) 猪
6. Your mobile's useless. 7. 吗 8. Because she doesn't like him. 9. c) 医生 10. There's no water in the fridge.

Lesson 1

1 1) d 2) b   2 1) 8 2) 11   3 推；拉

Lesson 2

1 1) c 入口 2) b 出口 3) a 出站

2 a e   3 1) 入口 2) 出口 3) 出站

Lesson 3

1 third from the top 2 1) b 2) a   3 c 间

Lesson 4

1 b   2 学

3 1) university 2) secondary school, middle school

4 1) 你的小学在哪？ Nǐ de xiǎo xué zài nǎr?

2) 你的大学在哪？ Nǐ de dà xué zài nǎr?

3) 他在上中学。 Tā zài shàng zhōng xué.

Lesson 5

1 b   2 1) d 2) b 3) c 4) a

Lesson 6

1 1) b 2) a 3) d 4) c   2 b cabd

Lesson 7

1 1) 酒 2) 餐 3) 餐 4) 饭 5) 面 6) 吃
2 duck   3 cadb

Glossaries

English-Hanzi-Pinyin

Use this glossary of the words and meanings used in the book if you already know the English and want to check the corresponding Chinese characters or pronunciation.

A

able: to be able to 能 néng

afternoon 下午 xià wǔ

again 又 yòu

all 都 dōu

all right: it's all right 没关系 méi guān xi

already 已经 yǐ jīng

also 也 yě

am 是 shì

America 美国 Měi guó

American (adjective) 美国 Měi guó; (person) 美国人 Měi guó rén

and 和 hé

apple 苹果 píng guǒ

April 四月 sì yuè

are 是 shì

to arrive 来 lái

to ask 问 wèn; 请 qǐng

at 在 zài; (as in smile at) 对 duì

August 八月 bā yuè

autumn 秋天 qiū tiān

B

back (part) 后 hòu; (of body) 背 bèi

bad 坏 huài

banana 香蕉 xiāng jiāo

bank (for money) 银行 yín háng

to be 是 shì

to be able to 会 huì

beautiful 美 měi

bed 床 chuáng

Beijing 北京 Běijīng

big 大 dà

bike 自行车 zì xíng chē

bird 鸟 niǎo

birthday 生日 shēngrì ;
happy birthday 生日快
乐 shēngrì kuàilè

black 黑 hēi

blue 蓝 lán

book 书 shū

both 都 dōu

bowl 碗 wǎn

boy 男孩（子） nán hái
(zi)

Brit 英国人 Yīng guó rén

Britain 英国 Yīng guó

British 英国 Yīng guó

bus 公共汽车 gōng gòng
qì chē

businessman 商人 shāng rén

C

can 能 néng;
(be permitted to) 可以 kě yǐ

car 汽车 qì chē

care: take care (as in 'bye,
take care) 多保重 duō bǎo
zhòng

carpet 地毯 dì tǎn

cat 猫 māo

chair 椅子 yǐ zi

character (in Chinese script)
字 zì

chicken 鸡 jī

child 孩子 hái zi

chin 下巴 xià ba

China 中国 Zhōng guó

Chinese (adjective) 中国
Zhōng guó;
(language) 中文 Zhōng
wén;
(person) 中国人 Zhōng
guó rén

Chinese character 汉字 hàn
zì

chopsticks 筷子 kuài zi

civil servant 公务员 gōng wù yuán

class (at school) 课 kè

classroom 课堂 kè táng

clothes 衣服 yī fu

cloud 云 yún

coat 大衣 dà yī

cold (adjective) 冷 lěng

colour 色 sè

to come 来 lái

to come back 回来 huí lái

computer 电脑 diàn nǎo

conversation 话 huà

correct 对 duì

cow 牛 niú

crow 乌鸦 wū yā

to cry 哭 kū

cup 杯子 bēi zi; a cup of … 一杯··· yì bēi…

D

dad 爸爸 bà ba

daughter 女儿 nǚ ér

day 天 tiān

December 十二月 shí'èr yuè

desk 桌子 zhuō zi

different 不同 bù tóng

dispensary 药房 yào fáng

divided by 除以 chú yǐ

to do 做 zuò

doctor 医生 yī shēng

dog 狗 gǒu

door 门 mén

duck 鸭 yā

E

ear 耳 ěr

early morning 早上 zǎo shàng

earth (soil) 土 tǔ

east 东 dōng

to eat 吃 chī

eight 八 bā

eighty 八十 bā shí

electric 电 diàn

eleven 十一 shí yī

emergency 急诊 jí zhěn

England 英国 Yīng guó

English *(adjective)* 英国 Yīng guó

entrance 入口 rù kǒu

equals 等于 děng yú

evening 晚上 wǎn shàng

excuse me 劳驾 láo jià

exit 出口 chū kǒu; *(from station)* 出站 chū zhàn

extremely 非常 fēi cháng

F

face 脸 liǎn

factory worker 工人 gōng rén

fairly 比较 bǐ jiào

farmer 农民 nóng mín

fast 快 kuài

father 父亲 fù qīn

February 二月 èr yuè

female 女 nǚ

festival 节 jié

few, fewer 少 shǎo

fifty 五十 wǔ shí

finally 最后 zuì hòu

fine *(good)* 好 hǎo

fire 火 huǒ

five 五 wǔ

floor 地板 dì bǎn

flower 花 huā

foot 脚 jiǎo

forest 森 sēn

fork 叉 chā

forty 四十 sì shí

four 四 sì

France 法国 Fǎ guó

French *(adjective)* 法国 Fǎ guó

Friday 星期五 xīng qī wǔ, 周五 zhōu wǔ

fridge 冰箱 bīng xiāng

from 从 cóng;
 I come from… 我从…来
 wǒ cóng…lái

front 前 qián;
 in front of 在…前边 zài
 … qián biān

fruit 水果 shuǐ guǒ

G

German (adjective) 德国 Dé
 guó

Germany 德国 Dé guó

girl 女孩（子）   nǚ hái
 (zi)

glass 杯子 bēi zi;
 a glass of … 一杯… yì
 bēi…

glove 手套 shǒu tào

to go 去 qù;
 to go back 回（去） huí
 (qù);
 to go home 回家 huí
 jiā

good 好 hǎo;

good afternoon 下午好
 xià wǔ hǎo;
good evening 晚上好
 wǎn shàng hǎo;
good morning 早上好 zǎo
 shàng hǎo;
good night 晚安 wǎn ān

goodbye 再见 zài jiàn

goose 鹅 é

granddaughter 孙女 sūn nǚ

grandfather 祖父 zǔ fù

grandma 奶奶 nǎi nai

grandmother 祖母 zǔ mǔ

grandpa 爷爷 yé ye

grandson 孙子 sūn zi

grass 草 cǎo

green 绿 lǜ

H

hair 头发 tóu fà;
 发 fà

half 半 bàn;
 half past 半 bàn

hand 手 shǒu

happy 快乐 kuàilè

to have 有 yǒu

to have to 得 děi;
必须 bì xū

he 他 tā

head 头 tóu

heart 心 xīn

hello 你好 nǐ hǎo

her 她 tā

here 这里 zhè lǐ

hers 她的 tā de

him 他 tā

his 他的 tā de

home 家 jiā

horse 马 mǎ

hospital 医院 yī yuàn

hot 热 rè

hour 小时 xiǎo shí

how? 怎么（样）？ zěn me
(yàng)?;
how many?; how much? 多
少? duō shǎo?

hundred 百 bǎi

hundred million 亿 yì

I

I 我 wǒ

ice 冰 bīng

in... 在···里 zài...lǐ

internet café 网吧 wǎng bā

to invite 请 qǐng

is 是 shì

it 它 tā

Italian *(adjective)* 意大利 Yì
dà lì

Italy 意大利 Yì dà lì

its 它的 tā de

J

jacket 上衣 shàng yī

January 一月 yī yuè

Japan 日本 Rì běn

Japanese *(adjective)* 日本 Rì
běn

job 工作 gōng zuò

judge 法官 fǎ guān

July 七月 qī yuè

June 六月 liù yuè

K

knife 刀 dāo

to know 知道 zhī dào;
(person, be acquainted with)
认识 rèn shi

L

lady 女士 nǚ shì

lamp 电灯 diàn dēng

land 土 tǔ

language 话 huà

last year 去年 qù nián

to laugh 笑 xiào

lawyer 律师 lǜ shī

to leave 走 zǒu

left (not right) 左 zuǒ

less 少 shǎo

lesson 课 kè

light 光 guāng

to like 喜欢 xǐ huān

long 长 cháng

to look at 看 kàn

lorry 卡车 kǎ chē

lots (of) 多 duō

lovely 美 měi

M

to make 做 zuò

male 男 nán

man 男人 nán rén

many 多 duō

March 三月 sān yuè

matter 事 shì;
it doesn't matter 没关系
méi guān xi

May 五月 wǔ yuè

may 可以 kě yǐ

me 我 wǒ

meal 餐 cān

to meet 见 jiàn

mention: don't mention it 不客气 bú kè qi

mind: never mind 没关系 méi guān xi

mine 我的 wǒ de

minus 减 jiǎn

minute 分 fēn

mobile phone 手机 shǒu jī

Monday 星期一 xīng qī yī, 周一 zhōu yī

monkey 猴 hóu

month 月 yuè

moon 月 yuè

moonlight 月光 yuè guāng

morning 上午 shàng wǔ

mother 母亲 mǔ qīn

mountain 山 shān

to move 走 zǒu

Mr 先生 Xiān shēng

Ms 女士 Nǚ shì

much 多 duō

multiplied by 乘以 chéng yǐ

mum 妈妈 mā ma

must 得 děi; 必须 bì xū

my 我的 wǒ de

N

to need 要 yào; 需要 xū yào

news 消息 xiāo xī

next 下 xià; next year 明年 míng nián

nice 好 hǎo

nine 九 jiǔ

ninety 九十 jiǔ shí

no 不 bù; no, I'm not/it isn't etc 不是 bú shì; there's no... 没有... méi yǒu...

noodles 面 miàn

noon 中午 zhōng wǔ

north 北 běi

not 不 bù; (with **yǒu** and past tense) 没 méi

notebook 笔记本 bǐ jì běn

November 十一月 shí yī yuè

nurse 护士 hù shi

O

o'clock 点 diǎn

October 十月 shí yuè

of 的 de;
the X of Y Y的 X

ok 好的 hǎo de

old 老 lǎo;
how old are you? 你多大了？nǐ duō dà le?

old person 老人 lǎo rén

older brother 哥哥 gē ge

older sister 姐姐 jiě jie

on... 在···上 zài...shàng

one 一 yī

orange 桔子 jú zi

ought to 应该 yīng gāi

our(s) 我们的 wǒ men de

outside 外 wài

P

pair 双 shuāng

paper 纸 zhǐ

pardon me 对不起 duì bù qǐ

particularly 特别 tè bié

payment 收费 shōu fèi

peach 桃子 táo zi

pear 梨 lí

pen 笔 bǐ

pencil 铅笔 qiān bǐ

period 期 qī

person 人 rén

piece 块 kuài;
piece of paper 纸 zhǐ

pig 猪 zhū

pink 粉 fěn

plane 飞机 fēi jī

plate 盘子 pán zi

please 请 qǐng

plus 加 jiā

policeman 警察 jǐng chá

pretty 美 měi

primary school 小学 xiǎo xué

problem: no problem 没问题 méi wèn tí

public phone 公用电话 gōng yòng diàn huà

to pull 拉 lā

purple 紫 zǐ

to push 推 tuī

Q

to query 问 wèn

R

rain 雨 yǔ;
  it's raining 下雨了 xià yǔ le

to read 看 kàn;
  I can read Chinese 我认识汉字 wǒ rèn shi hàn zì

to recognize 认识 rèn shi

red 红 hóng

to register 挂号 guà hào

relatively 比较 bǐ jiào

to require 需要 xū yào

to return 回 huí

rice 饭 fàn

right 对 duì;
  (not left) 右 yòu

river 河 hé

round trip 来回 lái huí

rubber 橡皮 xiàng pí

ruler 尺子 chǐ zi

S

Saturday 星期六 xīng qī liù,
  周六 zhōu liù

saucer 碟子 dié zi

to say 说 shuō

scenery 风光 fēng guāng

school 学校 xué xiào

secondary school 中学 zhōng xué

to see 看 kàn;
看见 kàn jiàn;
见 jiàn;
see you later 回头见 huí tóu jiàn;
see you tomorrow 明天见 míng tiān jiàn

September 九月 jiǔ yuè

seven 七 qī

seventy 七十 qī shí

Shanghai 上海 Shànghǎi

she 她 tā

sheep 羊 yáng

ship 船 chuán

shoe 鞋子 xié zi

short 短 duǎn

should 应该 yīng gāi

side 边 biān

sir 先生 xiān shēng

to sit 坐 zuò

to sit down 坐下 zuò xià

six 六 liù

sixty 六十 liù shí

sky 天 tiān

slow 慢 màn

small 小 xiǎo

to smile 笑 xiào

snow 雪 xuě;
it's snowing 下雪了 xià xuě le

sock 袜子 wà zi

soldier 军人 jūn rén

some 一些 yì xiē

son 儿子 ér zi

sorry 对不起 duì bù qǐ

south 南 nán

Spain 西班牙 Xī bān yá

Spanish (adjective) 西班牙 Xī bān yá

to speak 说话 shuō huà;
说 shuō

specially 特别 tè bié

speech 话 huà

spring 春天 chūn tiān

star 星 xīng

stone 石头 shí tóu

student 学生 xué shēng

summer 夏天 xià tiān

Sunday 星期天 xīng qī tiān,
周日 zhōu rì

sunlight 日光 rì guāng

swan 天鹅 tiān é

T

table 桌子 zhuō zi

to talk 说话 shuō huà;
说 shuō

taxi 出租车 chū zū chē

teacher 老师 lǎo shī

telephone 电话 diàn huà

television 电视 diàn shì

ten 十 shí;
ten thousand 万 wàn

textbook 课本 kè běn

thank you 谢谢 (你) xiè xiè (nǐ)

thanks a lot; thank you very much 非常感谢 fēi cháng gǎn xiè

that 那 nà;
that one 那个 nà ge

their(s) *(masculine)* 他们的 tā men de;
(feminine) 她们的 tā men de;
(inanimate) 它们的 tā men de

them *(masculine)* 他们 tā men;
(feminine) 她们 tā men;
(inanimate objects) 它们 tā men

then 然后 rán hòu

there 那里 nà lǐ;
there is, there are 有 yǒu;
there isn't, there aren't 没有 méi yǒu

these 这些 zhè xiē

they *(masculine)* 他们 tā men;
(feminine) 她们 tā men;
(inanimate objects) 它们 tā men

thing *(matter)* 事 shì

to think 想 xiǎng

thirteen 十三 shí sān

thirty 三十 sān shí

this 这 zhè;
  this one 这个 zhè ge

those 那些 nà xiē

thousand 千 qiān

three 三 sān

Thursday 星期四 xīng qī sì,
周四 zhōu sì

tiger 虎 hǔ

time: what time is it?
几点了？ jǐ diǎn le?

to (*as in 'say to'*) 对 duì

today 今天 jīn tiān

toilet 卫生间 wèi shēng
  jiān;
洗手间 xǐ shǒu jiān

tomorrow 明天 míng
  tiān;
  the day after tomorrow 后
天 hòu tiān

tongue 舌 shé

too 太 tài;
  (*also*) 也 yě

tooth 牙 yá

train 火车 huǒ chē

tree 树 shù

trousers 裤子 kù zi

Tuesday 星期二 xīng
  qī 'èr,
周二 zhōu 'èr

twelve 十二 shí èr

twenty 二十 èr shí

two (*number*) 二 èr;
  (*used with measure words*) 两
liǎng

U

ugly 丑 chǒu

under 下 xià

underground 地铁 dì tiě

university 大学 dà xué

us 我们 wǒ men

V

very 很 hěn

W

to walk 走 zǒu

to walk back 走回去 zǒu huí qù

to want 想 xiǎng; 要 yào

wardrobe 衣柜 yī guì

washing machine 洗衣机 xǐ yī jī

to watch 看 kàn

watch (*wristwatch*) 手表 shǒu biǎo

water 水 shuǐ

we 我们 wǒ men

Wednesday 星期三 xīng qī sān, 周三 zhōu sān

week 周 zhōu

welcome: you're welcome 不客气 bú kè qi

well: as well 也 yě

west 西 xī

what? 什么? shén me?; what's the matter with you?

你怎么了? nǐ zěn me le?; what's the matter? 怎么回事? zěn me huí shì?

when? 什么时候? shén me shí hòu?

where? 哪里? ná lǐ?; where do you come from? 你从哪里来? nǐ cóng nǎ lǐ lái?

which? 哪一个? nǎ yí gè?

white 白 bái

who? 谁? shéi?

whose? 谁的? shéi de?

why? 为什么? wèi shén me?

will 会 huì

wind 风 fēng

window 窗户 chuāng hu

wine 酒 jiǔ

winter 冬天 dōng tiān

wolf 狼 láng

woman 女人 nǚ rén

wood 木 mù

woods 林 lín

word 字 zì

to work 工作 gōng zuò;
做事 zuò shì

would like 想要 xiǎng
yào

to write 写 xiě
to write (Chinese) 写字 xiě
zì

writing 文 wén

wrong 错 cuò

Y

year 年 nián;
(in saying your age) 岁 suì;
this year 今年 jīn nián

yellow 黄 huáng

yesterday 昨天 zuó tiān

you *(singular)* 你 nǐ
(plural) 你们 nǐ men

younger brother 弟弟 dì di

younger sister 妹妹 mèi
mei

your(s) *(singular)* 你的 nǐ de
(plural) 你们的 nǐ men de

Z

zero 零 líng

Pinyin-Hanzi-English

Use this glossary of words and meanings that occur in the book if you know the pronunciation and want to check the Chinese characters or the English meaning.

Pinyin headwords are ordered according to the tone of the first pinyin word. The sequence is: no tone (or light tone), first (ˉ), second (´), third (ˇ), fourth (`).

A

ān 安 peace

B

bā 八 eight

bā shí 八十 eighty

bā yuè 八月 August

bǎ 把 measure word for things like rulers, scissors, knives, umbrellas; also chairs

bà ba 爸爸 dad

bái 白 white

bǎi 百 hundred

bàn 半 half; half past

bēi 杯 glass; cup

bēi zi 杯子 glass; cup

běi 北 north

Běijīng 北京 Beijing

bèi 背 back (of body)

běn 本 measure word for books and magazines

bǐ 笔 pen

bǐ jì běn 笔记本 notebook

bǐ jiào 比较 relatively, fairly

bì xū 必须 must; to have to

biān 边 side

bīng 冰 ice

bīng xiāng 冰箱 fridge

bù 不 no; not

bú kè qi 不客气 you're welcome; don't mention it

bú shì 不是 no; not; isn't; am not; aren't

bù tóng 不同 different

C

cān 餐 meal

cǎo 草 grass

chā 叉 fork

cháng 长 long

chē 车 bus; car

chéng yǐ 乘以 multiplied by

chī 吃 to eat

chǐ zi 尺子 ruler

chǒu 丑 ugly

chū kǒu 出口 exit

chū zhàn 出站 exit

chū zū chē 出租车 taxi

chú yǐ 除以 divided by

chuán 船 ship

chuāng hu 窗户 window

chuáng 床 bed

chūn 春 spring

chūn tiān 春天 spring

cóng 从 from

cuò 错 wrong

D

dà 大 big
nǐ duō dà le? 你多大了? how old are you?

dà xué 大学 university

dà yī 大衣 coat

dāo 刀 knife

de 的 of; used after an adjective coming before a noun

Dé guó 德国 Germany; German

děi 得 must, to have to

děng yú 等于 equals

dì di 弟弟 younger brother

dì bǎn 地板 floor

dì tǎn 地毯 carpet

dì tiě 地铁 underground

diǎn 点 o'clock

diàn 电 electric

diàn dēng 电灯 lamp

diàn huà 电话 telephone

diàn nǎo 电脑 computer

diàn shì 电视 television

dié zi 碟子 saucer

dōng 东 east

dōng 冬 winter

dōng tiān 冬天 winter

dōu 都 both; all

duǎn 短 short

duì 对 right; correct; to; at

duì bù qǐ 对不起 sorry; pardon me

duō 多 lots (of); many; much
　duō bǎo zhòng 多保重 take care
　duō shǎo? 多少? how many?; how much?

E

é 鹅 goose

ér zi 儿子 son

ěr 耳 ear

èr 二 two

èr shí 二十 twenty

èr yuè 二月 February

F

fǎ guān 法官 judge

Fǎ guó 法国 France; French

fà 发 hair

fàn 饭 rice

fēi cháng 非常 extremely; very
　fēi cháng gǎn xiè 非常感谢 thanks a lot; thank you very much

fēi jī 飞机 plane

fēn 分 minute

fěn 粉 pink

fēng 风 wind

fēng guāng 风光 scenery

fù qīn 父亲 father

G

gē ge 哥哥 older brother

gè 个 general purpose measure word

gōng rén 工人 factory worker

gōng zuò 工作 to work; job

gōng gòng qì chē 公共汽车 bus

gōng wù yuán 公务员 civil servant

gōng yòng diàn huà 公用电话 public phone

gǒu 狗 dog

guà hào 挂号 to register

guāng 光 light

guó 国 country

H

hái zi 孩子 child

hǎi 海 sea

hàn zì 汉字 Chinese character

hǎo 好 good; fine; nice

hǎo de 好的 ok

hào: 5 hào 五号 number 5

hé 和 and

hé 河 river

hēi 黑 black

hěn 很 very

hóng 红 red

hóu 猴 monkey

hòu 后 back

hòu tiān 后天 the day after tomorrow

hǔ 虎 tiger

hù shi 护士 nurse

huā 花 flower

huà 话 speech; language; conversation

huài 坏 bad

huáng 黄 yellow

huí 回 to return; to go back

huí jiā 回家 to go home

huí lái 回来 to come back

huí qù 回去 to go back

huí tóu jiàn 回头见 see you later

huì 会 will; to be able to

huǒ 火 fire

huǒ chē 火车 train

J

jī 鸡 chicken

jí zhěn 急诊 emergency

jǐ 几 how many
jǐ diǎn le? 几点了? what time is it?

jiā 家 home

jiā 加 plus

jiǎn 减 minus

jiàn 件 measure word for sweaters, tops, coats etc

jiàn 见 to see, to meet

jiǎo 脚 foot

jié 节 festival

jiě jie 姐姐 older sister

jīn nián 今年 this year

jīn tiān 今天 today

jǐng chá 警察 policeman

jiǔ 九 nine

jiǔ shí 九十 ninety

jiǔ yuè 九月 September

jiǔ 酒 wine

jú zi 桔子 orange

jūn rén 军人 soldier

K

kǎ chē 卡车 lorry

kàn 看 to look at, to see, to watch; to read

kàn jiàn 看见 to see

kè 课 class, lesson

kè běn 课本 textbook

kè táng 课堂 classroom

kě yǐ 可以 may; can

kū 哭 to cry

kù zi 裤子 trousers

kuài 快 fast

kuài 块 piece; block

kuài zi 筷子 chopsticks

kuàilè 快乐 happy

L

lā 拉 to pull

lái 来 to come; to arrive
nǐ cóng nǎ lǐ lái? 你从哪里来？ where do you come from?

lái huí 来回 round trip

lán 蓝 blue

láng 狼 wolf

láo jià 劳驾 excuse me

lǎo 老 old

lǎo rén 老人 old person

lǎo shī 老师 teacher

le 了 indicator for a completed action or a past event

lěng 冷 cold

lí 梨 pear

lǐ 里 in

liǎn 脸 face

liǎng 两 two

lín 林 woods

líng 零 zero

liù 六 six

liù shí 六十 sixty

liù yuè 六月 June

lǜ 绿 green

lǜ shī 律师 lawyer

M

ma 吗 question word

mā ma 妈妈 mum

mǎ 马 horse

màn 慢 slow

māo 猫 cat

méi 没 not; have not
méi guān xi 没关系 it's all right; it doesn't matter
méi wèn tí 没问题 no problem

méi yǒu 没有 not; have not; there isn't/aren't

měi 美 beautiful, pretty, lovely

Měi guó 美国 America; American

Měi guó rén 美国人 American

mèi mei 妹妹 younger sister

mén 门 door

miàn 面 noodles

mín 民 people

míng nián 明年 next year

míng tiān 明天 tomorrow

míng tiān jiàn 明天见 see you tomorrow

mǔ qīn 母亲 mother

mù 木 wood

N

ná lǐ? 哪里? where?

nǎ yí gè? 哪一个? which?

nà 那 that

nà ge 那个 that; that one

nà lǐ 那里 there

nà xiē 那些 those

nǎi nai 奶奶 grandma

nán 南 south

nán 男 male

nán hái 男孩 boy

nán hái zi 男孩子 boy

nán rén 男人 man

néng 能 can, to be able to

nǐ 你 you (singular)

nǐ de 你的 your; yours (singular)

nǐ hǎo 你好 hello

nǐ men 你们 you (plural)

nǐ men de 你们的 your; yours (plural)

nián 年 year

niǎo 鸟 bird

niú 牛 cow

nóng mín 农民 farmer

nǚ 女 female

nǚ ér 女儿 daughter

nǚ hái 女孩 girl

nǚ hái zi 女孩子 girl

nǚ rén 女人 woman

nǚ shì 女士 Ms, lady

P

pán zi 盘子 plate

pǐ 匹 measure word for horses

píng guǒ 苹果 apple

Q

qī 期 period

qī 七 seven

qī shí 七十 seventy

qī yuè 七月 July

qì chē 汽车 car

qiān 千 thousand

qiān bǐ 铅笔 pencil

qián 前 front

qǐng 请 please; to ask; to invite

qiū 秋 autumn

qiū tiān 秋天 autumn

qù 去 to go

qù nián 去年 last year

R

rán hòu 然后 then

rè 热 hot

rén 人 person

rèn shi 认识 to know; to recognize

wǒ rèn shi hàn zì 我认识汉字 I can read Chinese

rì 日 day

Rì běn 日本 Japan; Japanese

rì guāng 日光 sunlight

rù kǒu 入口 entrance

S

sān 三 three

sān shí 三十 thirty

sān yuè 三月 March

sè 色 colour

sēn 森 forest

sēn lín 森林 dense forest

shān 山 mountain

shàn 扇 measure word for windows

shāng rén 商人 businessman

shàng 上 on

shàng wǔ 上午 morning

shàng yī 上衣 jacket

Shànghǎi 上海 Shanghai

shǎo 少 few; fewer; less

shé 舌 tongue

shéi? 谁? who?

shéi de? 谁的? whose?

shén me? 什么? what?

shén me shí hòu? 什么时候? when?

shēngrì 生日 birthday
shēngrì kuàilè 生日快乐 happy birthday

shí 时 time

shí 十 ten

shí èr 十二 twelve

shí'èr yuè 十二月 December

shí sān 十三 thirteen

shí yī 十一 eleven

shí yī yuè 十一月 November

shí yuè 十月 October

shí tóu 石头 stone

shì 事 thing, matter

shì 是 to be; am, is, are

shōu fèi 收费 payment

shǒu 手 hand

shǒu biǎo 手表 watch

shǒu jī 手机 mobile phone

shǒu tào 手套 glove

shū 书 book

shù 树 tree

shuāng 双 pair

shuǐ 水 water

shuǐ guǒ 水果 fruit

shuō 说 to talk; to speak; to say

shuō huà 说话 to speak; to talk

sì 四 four

sì shí 四十 forty

sì yuè 四月 April

suì 岁 year

sūn nü 孙女 granddaughter

sūn zi 孙子 grandson

T

tā 他 he; him

tā 它 it

tā 她 she; her

tā de 她的 her; hers

tā de 他的 his

tā de 它的 its

tā men 他们 they; them (*masculine*)

tā men 她们 they; them (*feminine*)

tā men 它们 they; them (*inanimate objects*)

tā men de 他们的 their; theirs (*masculine*)

tā men de 她们的 their; theirs (*feminine*)

tā men de 它们的 their; theirs (*inanimate*)

tái 台 measure word for bigger machines

tài 太 too; very

táo zi 桃子 peach

tè bié 特别 particularly, specially

tiān 天 day; sky

tiān é 天鹅 swan

tóu 头 head; measure word for animals

tóu fà 头发 hair

tǔ 土 earth, soil; land

tuī 推 to push

W

wà zi 袜子 sock

wài 外 outside

wǎn 碗 bowl

wǎn ān 晚安 good night

wǎn shàng 晚上 evening
wǎn shàng hǎo 晚上好
good evening

wàn 万 ten thousand

wáng 王 king

wǎng bā 网吧 internet café

wèi 位 measure word for people with a specific profession

wèi shén me? 为什么? why?

wèi shēng jiān 卫生间 toilet

wén 文 writing; language

wèn 问 to ask; to query

wèn tí 问题 problem; question

wǒ 我 I; me

wǒ de 我的 my; mine

wǒ men 我们 we; us

wǒ men de 我们的 our; ours

wū yā 乌鸦 crow

wǔ 五 five

wǔ shí 五十 fifty

X

xī 西 west

Xī bān yá 西班牙 Spain; Spanish

xǐ huān 喜欢 to like

xǐ shǒu jiān 洗手间 toilet

xǐ yī jī 洗衣机 washing machine

xià 夏 summer

xià tiān 夏天 summer

xià 下 under; next
xià xuě le 下雪了 it's snowing
xià yǔ le 下雨了 it's raining

xià ba 下巴 chin

xià wǔ 下午 afternoon
xià wǔ hǎo 下午好 good afternoon

xiān shēng 先生 Mr, sir

xiāng jiāo 香蕉 banana

xiǎng 想 to think; to want

xiǎng yào 想要 would like

xiàng pí 橡皮 rubber

xiāo xī 消息 news

xiǎo 小 small

xiǎo shí 小时 hour

xiǎo xué 小学 primary school

xiào 笑 to laugh; to smile

xié zi 鞋子 shoe

xiě 写 to write

xiě zì 写字 to write (Chinese)

xiè xiè (nǐ) 谢谢 (你) thank you

xīn 心 heart

xīng 星 star

xīng qī 'èr 星期二 Tuesday

xīng qī liù 星期六 Saturday

xīng qī sān 星期三 Wednesday

xīng qī sì 星期四 Thursday

xīng qī tiān 星期天 Sunday

xīng qī wǔ 星期五 Friday

xīng qī yī 星期一 Monday

xū yào 需要 to need; to require

xuě 雪 snow

xué shēng 学生 student

xué xiào 学校 school

Y

yā 鸭 duck

yá 牙 tooth

yáng 羊 sheep

yào 要 to want; to need

yào fáng 药房 dispensary

yé ye 爷爷 grandpa

yě 也 also; too

yī 一 one

yī yuè 一月 January

yī fu 衣服 clothes

yī guì 衣柜 wardrobe

yī shēng 医生 doctor

yī yuàn 医院 hospital

yǐ jīng 已经 already

yǐ zi 椅子 chair

yì 亿 hundred million

Yì dà lì 意大利 Italy; Italian

yì xiē 一些 some

yín háng 银行 bank (for money)

yīng gāi 应该 should; must; ought to

Yīng guó 英国 Britain; England; British; English

Yīng guó rén 英国人 Brit

yòng 用 to use

yǒu 有 have, has, have got; there is; there are

yòu 又 again

yòu 右 right (not left)

yǔ 雨 rain

yuè 月 month; moon

yuè guāng 月光 moonlight

yún 云 cloud

Z

zài 在 at, in, on; present continuous tense indicator
tā zài gōng zuò 他在工作 he's working
zài...shàng 在···上 on, at
zài ... hòu biān 在···后边 behind
zài ... qián biān 在···前边 in front of

zài jiàn 再见 goodbye

zǎo shàng 早上 early morning
zǎo shàng hǎo 早上好 good morning

zěn me (yàng)? 怎么 (样)? how?
nǐ zěn me le? 你怎么了? what's the matter with you?
zěn me huí shì? 怎么回事? what's the matter?

zhāng 张 measure word for flat things like paper

zhè 这 this

zhè ge 这个 this; this one

zhè lǐ 这里 here

zhè xiē 这些 these

zhèng zài 正在 used to indicate continuous action

zhī 只 measure word for birds and animals

zhī 支 measure word for pens, pencils, cigarettes and long cylindrical things

zhī dào 知道 to know

zhǐ 纸 piece of paper

Zhōng guó 中国 China

Zhōng guó rén 中国人 Chinese (*person*)

Zhōng wén 中文 Chinese (*language*)

zhōng wǔ 中午 noon

zhōng xué 中学 secondary school

zhòng 重 heavy

zhōu 周 week

zhōu 'èr 周二 Tuesday

zhōu liù 周六 Saturday

zhōu rì 周日 Sunday

zhōu sān 周三 Wednesday

zhōu sì 周四 Thursday

zhōu wǔ 周五 Friday

zhōu yī 周一 Monday

zhū 猪 pig

zhuō zi 桌子 desk, table

zǐ 紫 purple

zǐ 子 child

zì 字 word; character

zì xíng chē 自行车 bike

zǒu 走 to walk; to leave; to move

zǒu huí qù 走回去 to walk back

zǔ fù 祖父 grandfather

zǔ mǔ 祖母 grandmother

zuì hòu 最后 finally

zuó tiān 昨天 yesterday

zuǒ 左 left

zuò 做 to do; to make

zuò 坐 to sit

zuò xià 坐下 to sit down

zuò shì 做事 to work

Hanzi-Pinyin-English

Use this glossary of the hanzi that occur in the book if you want to check the meaning or pronunciation of a Chinese character. Characters are organized according to their stroke count. To find a specific character, just count its strokes and then scan through the section with that number of strokes.

1 stroke

一 yī one

一月 yī yuè January

一些 yì xiē some

2 strokes

七 qī seven

七十 qī shí seventy

七月 qī yuè July

九 jiǔ nine

九十 jiǔ shí ninety

九月 jiǔ yuè September

了 le indicator for a completed action or a past event

二 èr two

二十 èr shí twenty

二月 èr yuè February

人 rén person

儿子 ér zi son

入口 rù kǒu entrance

八 bā eight

八十 bā shí eighty

八月 bā yuè August

几 jǐ how many

几点了? jǐ diǎn le? what time is it?

刀 dāo knife

十 shí ten

十一月 shí yī yuè November

十二月 shí'èr yuè December

十月 shí yuè October

又 yòu again

3 strokes

万 wàn ten thousand

三 sān three

三十 sān shí thirty

三月 sān yuè March

上 shàng on

上午 shàng wǔ morning

上衣 shàng yī jacket

上海 Shànghǎi Shanghai

下 xià under; next

下雨了 xià yǔ le it's raining

下雪了 xià xuě le it's snowing

下巴 xià ba chin

下午 xià wǔ afternoon

下午好 xià wǔ hǎo good afternoon

个 gè general purpose measure word

也 yě also; too

亿 yì hundred million

千 qiān thousand

卫生间 wèi shēng jiān toilet

叉 chā fork

土 tǔ earth, soil; land

大 dà big

你多大了? nǐ duō dà le? how old are you?

大衣 dà yī coat

大学 dà xué university

女 nǚ female

女人 nǚ rén woman

女儿 nǚ ér daughter

女士 nǚ shì Ms; lady

女孩（子） nǚ hái (zi) girl

子 zǐ child

小 xiǎo small

小时 xiǎo shí hour

小学 xiǎo xué primary school

山 shān mountain

工人 gōng rén factory worker

工作 gōng zuò to work; job

已经 yǐ jīng already

门 mén door

飞机 fēi jī aeroplane

马 mǎ horse

4 strokes

不 bù no; not

不同 bù tóng different

不客气 bú kè qi you're welcome, don't mention it

不是 bú shì no; not

丑 chǒu ugly

中 zhōng middle; China

中午 zhōng wǔ noon

中文 Zhōng wén Chinese *(language)*

中国 Zhōng guó China

中国人 Zhōng guó rén Chinese *(person)*

中学 zhōng xué secondary school

为什么？ wèi shén me? why?

乌鸦 wū yā crow

书 shū book

云 yún cloud

五 wǔ five

五十 wǔ shí fifty

五月 wǔ yuè May

什么？ shén me? what?

什么时候？ shén me shí hòu? when?

今天 jīn tiān today

今年 jīn nián this year

从 cóng from

你从哪里来？ nǐ cóng nǎ lǐ lái? where do you come from?

公务员 gōng wù yuán civil servant

公用电话 gōng yòng diàn huà public phone

公共汽车 gōng gòng qì chē bus

六 liù six

六十 liù shí sixty

六月 liù yuè June

分 fēn minute

匹 pǐ measure word for horses

双 shuāng pair

天 tiān day; sky

天鹅 tiān é swan

太 tài too; very

少 shǎo few; fewer; less

尺子 chǐ zi ruler

心 xīn heart

手 shǒu hand

手机 shǒu jī mobile phone

手表 shǒu biǎo watch

手套 shǒu tào glove

支 zhī measure word for pens, pencils, cigarettes and long cylindrical things

文 wén writing; language

日 rì day

日本 Rì běn Japan; Japanese

日光 rì guāng sunlight

月 yuè month; moon

月光 yuè guāng moonlight

木 mù wood

比较 bǐ jiào relatively, fairly

水 shuǐ water

水果 shuǐ guǒ fruit

火 huǒ fire

火车 huǒ chē train

父亲 fù qīn father

牙 yá tooth

牛 niú cow

王 Wáng Chinese surname; king

见 jiàn to see, to meet

认识 rèn shi to know; to recognize

我认识汉字 wǒ rèn shi hàn zì I can read Chinese

车 chē bus; car

长 cháng long

风 fēng wind

风光 fēng guāng scenery

Hanzi-Pinyin-English

5 strokes

东 dōng east

他 tā he; him

他们 tā men they; them (*masculine*)

他们的 tā men de their; theirs (*masculine*)

他的 tā de his

写 xiě to write

写字 xiě zì to write (Chinese)

冬 dōng winter

冬天 dōng tiān winter

出口 chū kǒu exit

出租车 chū zū chē taxi

出站 chū zhàn exit

加 jiā plus

北 běi north

北京 Běijīng Beijing

半 bàn half; half past

卡车 kǎ chē lorry

去 qù to go

去年 qù nián last year

发 fà hair

只 zhī measure word for birds and animals

可以 kě yǐ may; can

台 tái measure word for bigger machines

右 yòu right (*not left*)

号：五号 hào: 5 hào number 5

四 sì four

四十 sì shí forty

四月 sì yuè April

外 wài outside

头 tóu head; measure word for animals

头发 tóu fà hair

奶奶 nǎi nai grandma

它 tā it

它们 tā men they; them (*inanimate objects*)

它们的 tā men de their; theirs (*inanimate*)

Glossary

Hanzi-Pinyin-English

Glossary

它的 tā de its

对 duì right; correct; to; at

对不起 duì bù qǐ sorry; pardon me

左 zuǒ left *(not right)*

必须 bì xū must; to have to

本 běn measure word for books and magazines

正在 zhèng zài used to indicate continuous action

母亲 mǔ qīn mother

民 mín people

汉字 hàn zì Chinese character

生日 shēngrì birthday

生日快乐 shēngrì kuàilè happy birthday

用 yòng to use

电 diàn electric

电灯 diàn dēng lamp

电视 diàn shì television

电话 diàn huà telephone

电脑 diàn nǎo computer

白 bái white

石头 shí tóu stone

节 jié festival

边 biān side

鸟 niǎo bird

6 strokes

件 jiàn measure word for sweaters, tops, coats etc

会 huì will; to be able to

先生 xiān shēng Mr; sir

光 guāng light

再见 zài jiàn goodbye

军人 jūn rén soldier

农民 nóng mín farmer

冰 bīng ice

冰箱 bīng xiāng fridge

刘 Liú Chinese surname

吃 chī to eat

后 hòu back

后天 hòu tiān the day after tomorrow

吗 ma question word

回 huí to return; to go back

回去 huí qù to go back

回头见 huí tóu jiàn see you later

回来 huí lái to come back

回家 huí jiā to go home

在 zài at; present continuous tense indicator

在···上 zài … shàng on, at

在···后边 zài … hòu biān behind

在···前边 zài … qián biān in front of

地板 dì bǎn floor

地铁 dì tiě underground

地毯 dì tǎn carpet

多 duō lots (of); many; much

多少? duō shǎo? how many?; how much?

多保重 duō bǎo zhòng! take care!

她 tā she; her

她们 tā men they; them (feminine)

她们的 tā men de their; theirs (feminine)

她的 tā de her; hers

好 hǎo good; fine; nice

好的 hǎo de ok

妈妈 mā ma mum

字 zì word; character

孙 Sūn Chinese surname

孙女 sūn nü granddaughter

孙子 sūn zi grandson

安 ān peace

岁 suì year

年 nián year

收费 shōu fèi payment

早上 zǎo shàng early morning

早上好 zǎo shàng hǎo good morning

有 yǒu have, has, have got; there is; there are

朱 Zhū Chinese surname

爷爷 yé ye grandpa

百 bǎi hundred

红 hóng red

网吧 wǎng bā internet café

羊 yáng sheep

老 lǎo old

老人 lǎo rén old person

老师 lǎo shī teacher

耳 ěr ear

自行车 zì xíng chē bike

舌 shé tongue

色 sè colour

衣服 yī fu clothes

衣柜 yī guì wardrobe

西 xī west

西班牙 Xī bān yá Spain

那 nà that

那个 nà ge that; that one

那里 nà lǐ there

那些 nà xiē those

问 wèn to ask; to query

7 strokes

两 liǎng two

位 wèi measure word for people with a specific profession

你 nǐ you (singular)

你们 nǐ men you (plural)

你们的 nǐ men de your; yours (plural)

你好 nǐ hǎo hello

你的 nǐ de your; yours (singular)

冷 lěng cold

劳驾 láo jià excuse me

医生 yī shēng doctor

医院 yī yuàn hospital

吴 Wú Chinese surname

坏 huài bad

坐 zuò to sit

坐下 zuò xià to sit down

块 kuài piece; block

床 chuáng bed

应该 yīng gāi should; must; ought to

弟弟 dì di younger brother

张 zhāng measure word for flat things like paper; Chinese surname

快 kuài fast

快乐 kuàilè happy

我 wǒ I; me

我们 wǒ men we; us

我们的 wǒ men de our; ours

我的 wǒ de my; mine

把 bǎ measure word for things like rulers, scissors, knives, umbrellas; also for chairs

护士 hù shi nurse

时 shí time

李 Lǐ Chinese surname

来 lái to come; to arrive

来回 lái huí round trip

杨 Yáng Chinese surname

汽车 qì chē car

没 méi not; have not

没问题 méi wèn tí no problem

没关系 méi guān xi it's all right; it doesn't matter; never mind

没有 méi yǒu not; have not; there isn't/aren't

男 nán male

男人 nán rén man

男孩（子）nán hái (zi) boy

纸 zhǐ piece of paper; paper

花 huā flower

走 zǒu to walk; to leave; to move

走回去 zǒu huí qù to walk back

这 zhè this

这个 zhè ge this; this one

这里 zhè lǐ here

这些 zhè xiē these

里 lǐ in

陈 Chén Chinese surname

饭 fàn rice

鸡 jī chicken

8 strokes

事 shì thing, matter

周 zhōu week; Chinese surname

周一 zhōu yī Monday

周二 zhōu 'èr Tuesday

周三 zhōu sān Wednesday

周五 zhōu wǔ Friday

周六 zhōu liù Saturday

周日 zhōu rì Sunday

周四 zhōu sì Thursday

和 hé and

国 guó country

妹妹 mèi mei younger sister

姐姐 jiě jie older sister

学生 xué shēng student

学校 xué xiào school

拉 lā to pull

明天 míng tiān tomorrow

明天见 míng tiān jiàn see you tomorrow

明年 míng nián next year

杯 bēi glass; cup

杯子 bēi zi glass; cup

林 lín woods

河 hé river

法国 Fǎ guó France

法官 fǎ guān judge

爸爸 bà ba dad

狗 gǒu dog

的 de of; used after an adjective coming before a noun

知道 zhī dào know

英国 Yīng guó Britain; England; British; English

英国人 Yīng guó rén Brit

苹果 píng guǒ apple

虎 hǔ tiger

话 huà speech; language; conversation

雨 yǔ rain

非常 fēi cháng extremely; very

非常感谢 fēi cháng gǎn xiè thank you very much

9 strokes

前 qián front

南 nán south

哪一个? nǎ yí gè? which?

哪里? ná lǐ? where?

孩子 hái zi child

很 hěn very

律师 lǜ shī lawyer

怎么(样)? zěn me (yàng)? how?

你怎么了? nǐ zěn me le? what's the matter with you?

怎么回事? zěn me huí shì? what's the matter?

急诊 jí zhěn emergency

挂号 guà hào to register

星 xīng star

星期一 xīng qī yī Monday

星期二 xīng qī 'èr Tuesday

星期三 xīng qī sān Wednesday

星期五 xīng qī wǔ Friday

星期六 xīng qī liù Saturday

星期天 xīng qī tiān Sunday

星期四 xīng qī sì Thursday

春 chūn spring

春天 chūn tiān spring

昨天 zuó tiān yesterday

是 shì to be; am, is, are

树 shù tree

洗手间 xǐ shǒu jiān toilet

洗衣机 xǐ yī jī washing machine

点 diǎn o'clock

看 kàn to look at, to see, to watch; to read

看书 kàn shū to read a book

看见 kàn jiàn to see

祖父 zǔ fù grandfather

祖母 zǔ mǔ grandmother

秋 qiū autumn

秋天 qiū tiān autumn

美 měi beautiful, pretty, lovely

美国 Měi guó America; American

美国人 Měi guó rén American

背 bèi back (of body)

草 cǎo grass

药房 yào fáng dispensary

要 yào to want; to need

说 shuō to talk; to speak; to say

说话 shuō huà to speak; to talk

赵 Zhào Chinese surname

重 zhòng heavy

除以 chú yǐ divided by

面 miàn noodles

香蕉 xiāng jiāo banana

10 strokes

乘以 chéng yǐ multiplied by

哥哥 gē ge older brother

哭 kū to cry

夏 xià summer

夏天 xià tiān summer

家 jiā home

徐 Xú Chinese surname

扇 shàn measure word for windows

晚上 wǎn shàng evening
晚上好 wǎn shàng hǎo good evening

晚安 wǎn ān good night

桃子 táo zi peach

桌子 zhuō zi desk, table

桔子 jú zi orange

海 hǎi sea

消息 xiāo xī news

热 rè hot

特别 tè bié particularly, specially

狼 láng wolf

笑 xiào to laugh; to smile

笔 bǐ pen

笔记本 bǐ jì běn notebook

粉 fěn pink

能 néng can, to be able to

袜子 wà zi sock

请 qǐng please; to ask; to invite

课 kè class, lesson

课本 kè běn textbook

课堂 kè táng classroom

谁? shéi? who?

谁的? shéi de? whose?

都 dōu both; all

酒 jiǔ wine

铅笔 qiān bǐ pencil

鸭 yā duck

11 strokes

做 zuò to do; to make

做事 zuò shì to work

减 jiǎn minus

商人 shāng rén businessman

得 děi must, to have to

推 tuī to push

猪 zhū pig

猫 māo cat

盘子 pán zi plate

绿 lǜ green

梨 lí pear

脚 jiǎo foot

脸 liǎn face

船 chuán ship

银行 yín háng bank *(for money)*

雪 xuě snow

黄 huáng yellow; Chinese surname

12 strokes

喜欢 xǐ huān to like

最后 zuì hòu finally

期 qī period

森 sēn forest

森林 sēn lín dense forest

椅子 yǐ zi chair

然后 rán hòu then

猴 hóu monkey

短 duǎn short

窗户 chuāng hu window

等于 děng yú equals

紫 zǐ purple

裤子 kù zi trousers

谢谢（你） xiè xiè (nǐ) thank you

鹅 é goose

黑 hēi black

13 strokes

想 xiǎng to think; to want

想要 xiǎng yào would like

意大利 Yì dà lì Italy; Italian

碗 wǎn bowl

筷子 kuài zi chopsticks

蓝 lán blue

错 cuò wrong

零 líng zero

14 strokes

慢 màn slow

碟子 dié zi saucer

需要 xū yào to need; to require

15 strokes

德国 Dé guó Germany; German

橡皮 xiàng pí rubber

鞋子 xié zi shoe

16 strokes

餐 cān meal

19 strokes

警察 jǐng chá policeman